Warrior • 94

Polish Winged Hussar
1576–1775

Richard Brzezinski • Illustrated by Velimir Vuksic

First published in Great Britain in 2006 by Osprey Publishing,
Midland House, West Way, Botley, Oxford OX2 0PH, UK
443 Park Avenue South, New York, NY 10016, USA
E-mail: info@ospreypublishing.com

A CIP catalogue record for this book is available from the British Library

ISBN-10: 1 84176 650 X
ISBN-13: 978 1 84176 650 8

Page layout by Ken Vail Graphic Design, Cambridge, UK
Index by Alan Thatcher
Typeset in Helvetica and New Baskerville
Originated by PPS Grasmere, Leeds, UK
Printed in China through World Print Ltd.

06 07 08 09 10   10 9 8 7 6 5 4 3 2 1

FOR A CATALOGUE OF ALL BOOKS PUBLISHED BY OSPREY MILITARY AND
AVIATION PLEASE CONTACT:

NORTH AMERICA
Osprey Direct, c/o Random House Distribution Center, 400 Hahn Road,
Westminster, MD 21157
E-mail: info@ospreydirect.com

ALL OTHER REGIONS
Osprey Direct UK, P.O. Box 140 Wellingborough, Northants, NN8 2FA, UK
E-mail: info@ospreydirect.co.uk

www.ospreypublishing.com

Author's note

Although the history of the Polish 'winged' hussar spans
nearly three centuries, for reasons of space this book
concentrates on their heyday from 1576 to 1709. The term
'Polish' is used (with apologies) to cover all the diverse
ethnicities of the Polish–Lithuanian Commonwealth. Not
wishing to inflict Polish grammar on innocent readers, I
have occasionally Anglicized the plural endings of some
Polish words. For a general background to the army of this
period see R. Brzezinski, *Polish Armies 1569–1696*, 2 vols,
Osprey MAA 184 & 188 (1987). All translations from source
texts are by the author, and all images are from the author's
collection unless specially credited.

Author's acknowledgements

This book is the product of nearly 20 years of research in
Poland and throughout northern and central Europe, largely
from primary sources. There is much new material and
many images previously unseen even in Poland. Over the
years I have benefited from conversations with some of
Poland's leading military historians, including Zdzislaw
Zygulski, Jerzy Teodorczyk, Miroslaw Nagielski and Robert
I. Frost. In Sweden assistance was provided by Arne
Danielsson, Eva Turek, Fred Sandstedt and Lena Engquist-
Stanstedt of the Armémuseum, Nils Drejholt of the
Livrustkammaren, and in England by Danuta Szewczyk-
Prokurat at the Fawley Court Museum. I also wish to thank
Andrzej Dzieciolowski and Bohdan Wróblewski for details
relating to the Stockholm roll, and re-enactors from the
Zagloba's Tavern Yahoo group for practical advice on the
construction of hollow lances.
My warmest thanks go to John Rohde and Keith Roberts
for suggestions that have greatly improved the book, and to
Nick Sekunda for his moral support over many years, as
well as generous assistance in taming the text, and to
Joanna de Vries of Osprey for her hard work and saintly
patience in bringing this book into reality.

Dedication

For Zofia Stepkowska. In memory of Jerzy Teodorczyk
1930–2005, an inspirational historian at the Polish Army
Museum in Warsaw, who always had time for everyone.

CONTENTS

POLISH WINGED HUSSAR 1576–1775

INTRODUCTION

It would be futile to tell of the grandeur and beauty of this cavalry; to speak of their costumes, their tall lances with long pennants, their tiger skins and exquisite horses with saddles, stirrups and reins dripping with gold, embroidery and precious stones; to do so would only diminish their beauty. It is a chivalry that has no equal in the world; without seeing it with your own eyes, its vigour and splendour is impossible to imagine. (Italian envoy Cosimo Brunetti, after witnessing Sobieski's coronation parade in 1676)

The Polish 'winged' hussar was certainly among the most spectacular soldiers of all time. To Poles he is much more – a symbol of justifiable pride in military achievements and of a bygone age when the Polish–Lithuanian Commonwealth was geographically the largest nation of Europe, stretching from the Baltic almost to the Black Sea.

The Polish hussars have become the stuff of legend, but as with many national traditions (like the Highland clan tartan), many facets of their story were greatly embellished in the 19th century. The most obvious case in point is the wings. Modern illustrators habitually depict the hussars with pairs of colossal wings that arch forward over the head. Yet such wings leave hardly a trace in contemporary art. As we shall see, the

BELOW **Winged hussars charge during Jerzy Hoffman's filming of Sienkiewicz's epic *With Fire & Sword* (1998), set during the Ukrainian Cossack Rebellion of 1648–54. The author worked as a consultant on this production, and there was much discussion on the type of wing to be worn by the hussars. Despite extraordinary efforts to ensure historical accuracy in other parts of the film, audience expectations triumphed over history and the hussars were shown with the 'classic' forward curving wings, probably used only from the final decades of the 17th century.**

inescapable reality is that in the era of great victories (1577–c.1621) the hussars wore a less spectacular saddle-mounted wing. Similarly, it may alarm some to discover that most of the highly decorative suits of hussar armour that fill Poland's museums were not used during the 'golden age' of the hussars, but date from the 1630s and later.

It is also time to reassess one or two other accepted 'facts' about the Polish hussars – for example that these heavily armoured horsemen were able to change formation during a charge and, thanks to their extra-long lances, to ride, almost nonchalantly, over pike-armed infantry. Such claims are sheer fantasy.

Nevertheless, the Polish hussars were exceptional. Most European nations abandoned the heavy lancer soon after 1600, but the Poles continued to employ them with some success right up to the Great Northern War of 1700–21. This is a phenomenon that needs explaining.

The object of this book, then, is not to 'diminish the beauty' of the hussars, but rather to show them as they really looked, lived and fought, 'warts and all'. Thus the basic equipment of ordinary hussars is shown, not the jewelled weapons and *karacena* scale armour of senior officers. Even so, there is more than enough splendour to go round.

OUTLINE HISTORY OF THE HUSSAR

The Polish hussar was a hybrid, the offspring of a complicated mix of eastern and western ancestry. The armies of medieval Poland by and large had been western in character, with the lance-armed knight (*kopijnik*) in plate armour forming their backbone. This began to change as Poland established dynastic links with Lithuania – then a vast state that sprawled into the Russian steppe, with an army shaped by Mongol, Russian and Byzantine practices. After the Union of Lublin in 1569, Poland and Lithuania became a 'Commonwealth' (*Rzeczpospolita*), ruled by a single elected king and one parliament (the Seym) but fielding independent armies. Strong new tendencies were felt in the 16th century as the Commonwealth's southern borders came under threat from the Ottoman Turks. The once-powerful Serbian and Hungarian realms had already been consumed by the Ottoman advance, but centuries of Balkan resistance had fashioned a new troop type that was to survive and thrive in Poland – the hussar.

It was once believed that the first hussars were Hungarians recruited from one in 20 peasants (named from *húsz*, meaning 20), and fighting in a style copied from the Turks. But their origins go back much further. Tenth-century Byzantine military manuals mention light cavalry known as *chosarioi* or *chonsarioi*, recruited from Balkan peoples, especially Serbs, and 'ideal for scouting and raiding'. Their name, now routinely translated by Byzantine historians as 'hussar', probably derives in turn from *cursores* – 'runners', a late Roman class of light cavalry.

This Balkan light cavalry survived the shrinking of the Byzantine empire, though the Serbian articulation of their name, *gusar*, took on

ABOVE **Unarmoured Polish hussar from the ornamental border of a print showing Henri de Valois travelling to accept the Polish crown in 1573–74. He wears hose-like trousers and Hungarian ankle-boots and carries a *kopia* lance, painted with snake motif. The asymmetric 'Balkan' shield – reversed in error by the engraver – bears an *imprese* device as used in tournaments. Copy made in 1859 by Charles Tamisier of an engraving by Tobias Stimmer (1539–84).**

the nuance of 'bandit'. In the 14th century the medieval Serbian state, known as Rascia after its heart at the fortress of Ras (modern Novi Pazar), fell to the Turks, many 'Rascian' *gusars* found refuge in Hungary where they helped defend the southern border against the advancing Ottomans. The Hungarians spelt their name as *huszár*.

Early hussars in Poland

The first hussars to appear in Poland were also Serbians (Polish *Rac*). In 1500 several individual 'Rascians', each with a small retinue, appear in the pay records of the army of the royal court. Recruitment was quickly extended to Hungarians, Poles and Lithuanians, and in December 1501 the first full companies of *hussarorum alias raczew* were raised. Their name in Polish was usually spelt *usar*, less often *husar*. The term *husaria* soon emerged in army registers – alongside *cavalleria* – as a collective plural form.

The hussars of the Serbian style were unarmoured, relying on a large asymmetric 'Balkan' shield for defence and a light lance for attack, and were identical in appearance to the Stradiots or 'Albanians' in Venetian service (recruited, in fact, throughout the Balkans). They were quickly replaced by an armoured Hungarian style of hussar, which had emerged under the influence of Turkish *sipahi* cavalry in the early decades of the 16th century. In Poland these 'heavy' hussars were described by the acronym 'p.p.t.d.' – *pancerz, przylbica, tarcza, drzewo* (mail-shirt, helmet, shield, lance). Hussars armed in this manner formed 56 per cent of the cavalry at Jan Tarnowski's splendid victory over the Moldavians at Obertyn (1531). In Poland western influence remained stronger than in Hungary and until the 1550s hussar companies included a diminishing percentage of lancers, fully armoured in western style, alongside the hussars, who themselves often wore western items of armour.

In 1576 the Transylvanian prince Stefan Batory (Báthory) was elected king of Poland. He standardized the equipment of Polish hussars to conform with his personal guard of 400–500 Transylvanian and Hungarian hussars. The Balkan shield was abandoned and most hussars now had metal breastplates. The new model of hussar (see Plate A) was adopted throughout Polish and Lithuanian armies by the 1590s.

Heyday of the Polish hussar

At the battle of Lubieszów/Liebschau (1577) during the Danzig rebellion, King Stefan Batory's heavy hussar immediately proved itself a battle winner. He followed up with a series of victories over the Muscovite Russians (1579–82). Further successes came at Byczyna/Pitschen (1588) against a Habsburg army, and Bukow/Bucou (1600) over the Moldavians. Hussars now formed 75 per cent or more of the cavalry and seemed invincible on the eastern battlefield. Their greatest triumph was a series of dramatic victories against overwhelming odds over the Swedes at Kokenhusen (1601), Weissenstein (1604) and Kircholm (1605), and against a Russo-Swedish force at Kluszyn/Klushino (1610).

BELOW **Shields of this asymmetric shape were the standard equipment of early 16th-century hussars. They were known by the Turks as 'Rumelian' (i.e. Balkan) shields, by the Italians as Bosnian shields, and by Poles as Albanian or Hungarian shields. The 'winged-claw' device appears in central European heraldry, and evidently inspired some horsemen to tack actual wings on to the shields. When shields were abandoned these wings seem to have quickly evolved into the stylized 'wings' worn by Polish hussars.**

In the 1620s, however, the hussars suffered a crisis of confidence when facing the devastating firepower of the Swedish army newly reformed by Gustavus Adolphus. In response, the Poles recruited greater numbers of lighter cavalry and western-style infantry and by 1630 hussars rarely formed more than 30 per cent of the cavalry. The hussar's ascendancy was further challenged during a series of foreign invasions and civil wars that began in 1648. The Ukrainian Cossack Rebellion of 1648–54 was especially traumatic, and the hussars proved to be of limited value against the huge wagon-forts employed by the Ukrainians and the fast cavalry of their Tatar allies. At Batoh (1652) the veteran core of the *husaria* were captured and executed. About 1,000 hussars were recruited as replacements, but for the next 15 years the formation was a shadow of its former grandeur. During the 'Bloody Deluge' (1654–60) Poland was invaded by Swedes, Russians, Ukrainians, Brandenburgers and even Transylvanians. Swedish firepower again proved overwhelming. Against the Russians, however, the hussars' lances continued to be effective, contributing to the victories of the 'Fortunate Year' of 1660.

The Turks too remained vulnerable to the lance. Jan Sobieski, first as Crown Hetman, then as king (1674–96), oversaw the re-nationalizing of the army to face the Ottoman menace, and raised many new hussar companies, some by 'hussarifying' existing units of lighter cavalry. In an address to the Seym he called the hussars the 'hardwood of the army *robur militiae* … both an ornament and a defence … which no nation other than the Polish has, nor can ever have' (*WZ* 6, p. 78). Sobieski's cheerful gallantry prompted a new confidence among his hussars, and they won a string of victories over the Turks and their Tatar auxiliaries, and when he marched to the relief of Vienna (1683) it was 'with the bravest cavalry that the Sun ever beheld' (*Scanderbeg Redivivus*, 1684, p. 141).

Vienna was to be the hussars' last great victory. The long Turkish war that drew to a close in 1699 had crippled the Polish economy: many troops received no pay for over a decade. The hussars were to fight again in the Great Northern War (1700–21), but undermined by the machinations of powerful neighbours the Polish state slipped rapidly into anarchy, and the hussars no longer had the discipline nor the will to make a difference. Nevertheless, the hussars survived most of the 18th century more spectacular than ever, albeit as a militarily irrelevant parade formation.

ABOVE **Unarmoured Lithuanian hussar with huge asymmetric shield, striped *kopia* lance, and heron or egret feathers in the cap and ostrich plumes on the horse's head. From Abraham De Bruyn's costume book *Diversarium Gentium Armatura Equestri*, the first plates of which are dated 1575. His lack of armour has led some to suggest this is a very early hussar or even a light horseman; the answer is much simpler – metal armour is impractical in sub-zero winter weather.**

RECRUITMENT AND ORGANIZATION

The Polish hussars were organized along lines that were essentially medieval – derived from the same recruitment system formalized in the French *Ordonnances* of the 14th century. The basic company-sized unit in Poland was first known as a *rota*, from the French *rote* or *route*, a contingent raised by a single nobleman. The French combined small *rotes* into *bannières* of 100 for field service, and a similar practice survived in 16th-century Poland, where small *rotas* were combined to form a *choragiew*, literally 'banner'. By 1600, however, *rota* and *choragiew* had become synonymous – both now meant 'company'.

Rotmistrz and towarzysz

The commander or captain of a company was called a **rotmistrz** – 'rota-master'. He was normally a nobleman, from a land-owning class (*possessionati*) who at a minimum owned several villages, his wealth ensuring that the Seym did not immediately have to pay the entire cost of raising a unit. Many *rotmistrze* were wealthy magnates who further subsidized their companies to create an impressive bodyguard. Each of the two Polish and two Lithuanian hetmans (generals) maintained a hussar company and drew pay as its *rotmistrz*.

The *rotmistrz*'s contract was known as a 'letter of recruitment' (*list przypowiedni*) – analogous to the medieval French *lettre de retenue*. It was normally signed by the king, and commissioned the *rotmistrz* to raise a company of a specified strength, usually 100, 120 or 150 horses. Companies raised by hetmans and wealthier magnates could number 200 or even 300 horses.

The *rotmistrz* raised his company by contacting a number of **towarzysze** or 'companions'. Each of these assembled a **poczet** (retinue), the equivalent of the medieval 'lance', to serve with him. The *poczet* comprised, besides the *towarzysz*, a number of **pacholiks** or 'retainers' – as many as seven in the 16th century, falling to two in the 17th, and one by the 18th century – plus an unspecified number of camp servants who did not appear on the unit strength. The *towarzysz* was in a very real way a 'companion' of the *rotmistrz* – sharing the economic risk of raising the troops, and then serving alongside him on campaign.

The *towarzysz* was normally a nobleman. The Polish nobility or *szlachta* made up 6–8 per cent of the population, and claimed to be equals, but were separated by vast differences in wealth. Many poorer noblemen could not afford their own horse, and only middle and high-ranking nobles had the funds to outfit themselves as hussars. Those who did so often enlisted out of a genuine feeling of patriotic obligation and a desire to protect the homeland, but hussar service was also an excellent means of social advancement, the first step on a political career path, and a way of getting noticed in higher circles. The typical

BELOW **A company of winged hussars of a member of the Radziwill family on parade. Costume details suggest an early 18th-century date (not c.1680 as frequently stated). The unit comprises ten *towarzysze* (who march before the flag), an officer and a standard-bearer, three trumpeters and a kettledrummer, and 20 retainers (in plainer equipment). Detail of a print from the collection of W. Lozinski, published in his book *Zycie polskie w dawnych wiekach* (1912).**

length of service was three to five years. Wealthier individuals might purchase a place in the prestigious companies of the king or a hetman, enlisting for very short periods of just three months to one year, enough to give them the cachet of a 'soldier-knight'. Younger sons, with little chance of inheritance, tended to serve for longer, becoming career soldiers. In difficult times, men of uncertified pedigree and non-nobles might also be accepted as *towarzysze*, if they had the funds.

Hussar *towarzysze* entered an elite fraternity. Every nobleman expected to be addressed as *pan* ('lord' or 'sir'), but *towarzysze, rotmistrze* and hetmans called each other *pan brat* – 'my lord-brother'. To be a *towarzysz* of hussars conferred an exalted status in society at large. As the 18th-century memoirist Kitowicz commented: 'When all doors were shut to persons of lesser distinction at operas, balls or the royal chambers, *towarzysze* were always permitted to enter.'

The hussar *towarzysz* was a junior officer of sorts, but considered himself a cut above officers of the western model, particularly of dragoons and infantry, and could ignore their orders with impunity. When the *husaria* was abolished in 1775, the *towarzysz* became legally equivalent to *chorazy* (ensign) in units of the western model (*VL* 8, f.155).

Retainers and camp servants

By the 1630s the typical *towarzysz* received pay for three 'horses' or fighting men. Out of that money he raised a *poczet*, a small train or retinue, related in meaning to a military 'post' or 'watch', which consisted of himself plus two retainers or *pacholiks*. The *pacholik*, an obsolete spelling of *pacholek* ('youth'), might be a member of the impoverished nobility, though most were from the lower, non-noble classes. Foreigners referred to them as valets, squires or servants – hinting at the unequal relationship between *towarzysz* and *pacholik*. The *towarzysz* had complete jurisdiction over his *pacholiks*. Their names were not even recorded on the company roll. He could hire and fire them at will, and owned their equipment and horses. Some *pacholiks* were clearly treated as slaves, receiving little or no pay, and occasionally deserted, taking the master's valuable horses with them.

In the late 17th century the term *pacholik* began to be replaced by *pacholik poczytowy*, or simply **poczytowy** ('of the *poczet*'). Modern authors habitually use the term *poczytowy* for the entire period, or the still more anachronistic *szeregowy* ('of the ranks'), which came into use in the 18th century.

ABOVE **Polish hussars from Booth's**
Journael of 1632. At top
is a *towarzysz*, with single 'frame'
wing mounted on the saddle
(normally on the left, but the
engraving appears to be reversed).
His helmet with prominent
nasal bar is adorned with ostrich
feathers, as is the horse. He
wears a plate gauntlet on the bridle
hand. His swords are a Hungarian-
style sabre with long quillons, and
a *koncerz*, stowed under the thigh.
Altogether less impressive is the
retainer (*pacholik*) below, wearing
an unplumed *kapalin* helmet with
segmented cheekpieces, and riding
a cheaper horse, with only a small
blanket and simple stirrups.

The army was one of the few routes for social advancement. If a *pacholik* was able to acquire the necessary funds and horses, he could become a *towarzysz* in a lesser status unit of *pancerny–kozak* cavalry, where pedigree was often overlooked. The more successful *towarzysz* of *pancerny* cavalry might in turn enlist as a hussar.

The *towarzysz* also engaged **camp servants** to look after the wagons, tents and horses of his *poczet*. These were known as *ciury* (singular *ciura*) or *czeladz luzna* ('loose servants'). Westerners had difficulty grasping the difference between *pacholiks* and camp servants, which was not helped by the hussars' own habit of referring to the *pacholiks* and servants collectively as *czeladz* (singular *czeladnik*, 'apprentice').

The vast majority of camp servants were male. Army regulations forbade unmarried women from entering camp, and the noble wives of hussars would rarely deign to enter such surroundings. The wives of some poorer soldiers were less fussy, although several commanders, such as Jan Zamoyski in the 1580s, temporarily forbade the presence even of these. Sutlers and other females, including prostitutes, were always forced to live outside camp.

Since camp servants were not listed on the company registers it is difficult to quantify their numbers. Writers of the time estimate from one camp servant per fighting man to as many as four. A reliable figure is given by the engineer Naronowicz–Naronski (1659), who in his designs for the layout of military camps stated that each hussar company required space for 'the same again or even double the number of loose servants' – in other words, one to two servants per fighting man.

Junior company staff

The *rotmistrz* was assisted in his duties by a **porucznik** or lieutenant. Originally this officer was elected by the *towarzysze* from among their number; later he was contracted directly by the *rotmistrz* as his second. At first most *rotmistrze* personally led their companies to war, and even those who were wealthy magnates accompanied the army on campaign. By the 1630s many such VIPs never served in the field, and the hussar *rotmistrz* was now an honorary post, resembling the German *Inhaber* or owner-proprietor. The *porucznik*, a professional soldier, was now the actual commander. Though semantically equivalent to lieutenant, it was a far more important rank. The *porucznik* of a hetman's or royal company had particularly high status and often commanded an entire army division. From 1775 a hussar *porucznik* became legally equivalent to the colonel of a western-style formation.

Though the post of *towarzysz* carried prestige, that of *porucznik* was a huge step up the ladder, opening the way to a senior military rank and a civil career. The seniority of a *towarzysz* increased the higher up his name was listed on the muster roll, and the closer he came to promotion to *porucznik*. The position on the roll was fiercely contested, and was a frequent cause of duels.

The hussar *porucznik* was himself often called upon to perform higher command functions, and by the late 17th century he often left his unit in charge of a 'temporary lieutenant' or **namiestnik** (literally 'place-holder'). The **chorazy** (standard-bearer) for the company was usually selected from among the younger, more promising *towarzysze*, not necessarily one with experience – the post carried few executive powers. In the absence of the *porucznik*, command of the company often passed to a senior *towarzysz* rather than to the *chorazy*, and a senior *towarzysz* would often be promoted first.

There was no fixed requirement for musicians, though a **kettle-drummer** and several **trumpeters** were often present on the company register, especially in royal and magnatial companies. On the Stockholm roll of 1605, Gostomski's hussar company is shown with six musicians, for a unit described as 100 strong. The military reformer Aleksander Fredro proposed (in 1670) that these excessive musicians should be replaced so that each company had its own chaplain, barber-surgeon, locksmith (to repair firearms) and blacksmith. This would have brought the company staff up to par with units of western type such as dragoons, but was never implemented. **Chaplains** and **barber-surgeons** do sometimes appear on the company rolls, but their presence was optional; other providers of specialist skills are rarely listed. Such services were provided informally by camp servants and *pacholiks* who had been craftsmen in civilian life. For example, the hussar diarist Poczobut-Odlanicki mentions a certain Jurkowski (the surname of a noble), 'a very good tailor' who was serving in his *poczet* in 1660. Similarly, many staff functions were replaced by an assembly of the company's *towarzysze* and officers, known as the *kolo* (circle). This acted as an advisory council for the *rotmistrz* and as a court for the company.

Mustering and pay

A hussar company entered service, much as in any army of the period: the men were lined up before army commissioners, who entered the names of each *towarzysz* on to a company register, along with the number of mounted soldiers in his retinue (*poczet*). The company was then sworn in before its standard. The company register (or 'muster roll') was written down periodically and took the following form:

Register of the hussar rota of the Voivode of Kraków, Crown Grand Hetman [Stefan Potocki], beginning 1 April until the last of June 1658:

Poczet of the *rotmistrz*	24 horses
porucznik	6 horses
chorazy	4 horses
Suchodolski Jan	3 horses
Izdebski	3 horses

ABOVE **Polish hussar from the pamphlet *Pobudka zacnych synow* (Reveille to worthy sons) (1620), which calls on patriotic nobles to volunteer for service against the Turkish menace. Attached to his *kapalin* helmet is a helmet-wing (*forga*), worn instead of any other type of wing. Only mail sleeves are shown: armguards (*karwasze*) were just becoming popular. His *koncerz* sword hangs at an oblique angle, apparently from the saddle pommel.**

[48 further *towarzysze* with 3 horses;
2 *towarzysze* with 2 horses]
Total   188 horses

This company had a theoretical strength of 200 horses according to the 'letter of recruitment', but would be paid for 188 'horses' according to the register. The *poczet* of the *rotmistrz-Inhaber* often did not exist in reality, and this company was probably weaker still, numbering just 164 fighting men. Here the *rotmistrz* (Hetman Potocki) was allowed 24 'horses' for a 200-horse unit (12 for a 100-horse unit), the pay for which disappeared into his pocket. This was not a corrupt practice, merely a mechanism for covering officers' pay and other expenses. The *porucznik* (the actual commander) and the *chorazy* probably did have the four to six horses they were listed with, but even so the unit's real strength was nearly 13 per cent short of the official figures. By the late 17th century, perhaps 8–12 per cent of the 'horses' of the Polish cavalry as a whole existed only on paper.

The hussar's salary stood at 15 *zloty* in the 1570s and 1580s (18 *zloty* for hussars of the Court Army), paid quarterly, for each 'horse' of his *poczet*. Pay rose gradually in the early 17th century: from 20 *zloty*, to 30, then 40 and 50 *zloty*, fluctuating wildly during times of crisis, but rarely keeping up with inflation. However, from the mid-1650s until 1717, salary remained static at 51 *zloty*, despite being more than halved in value by inflation (although a wartime supplement of about 10 *zloty* quarterly was added from the 1690s).

These were not the only payments received. The *rotmistrz* was paid *kuchenne* (Latin *culinaria*) or 'kitchen money', amounting to 150 *zloty* per quarter for a 100-horse unit. By the mid-17th century this was absorbed into the pay, giving the peculiar extra *zloty* on the figures. A 'winter allowance' called *hiberna* covered the costs of living in quarters. From *c.*1650 this was legally extractable from the host population – and often was, at gunpoint. *Hiberna* could easily double the hussar's salary, and as state debts mounted in the later 17th century, it became the only cash regularly received.

State-paid, royal and private units

The same general scheme for raising hussars applied to all the professional (*zaciezne*) army units. The state-paid army consisted of two parts. Firstly, the standing army or **Kwarciani** ('Quarter troops'), named after the fraction (actually one-fifth) of the royal revenues set aside to pay them from 1563. They were normally stationed in the south-east guarding against Tatar incursions, and their 3–5,000 strength included about 1,000 hussars. Secondly there

BELOW **A Polish parade horse with a pair of saddle-mounted wings during the 'carousel' held in Stockholm to mark the coming of age of Carl XI in December 1672. Each wing is made from ostrich feathers inserted into a tubular shaft, which is secured to the side of the saddle by a double loop. This horse furniture was all probably looted in Poland during the 1655–56 campaign. (Later copy after an engraving by G.C. Eimmart in Ehrenstrahl's *Certamen equestre*, Stockholm, 1685)**

were 'supplementary' units raised in time of crisis after the Seym had voted funds: these made up the bulk of wartime armed forces. In 1652 after most of the *Kwarciani* were destroyed at the battle of Batoh, the Seym introduced a unified system of **Komputowe** troops, so called after the *Komput* or *état* (state) at which the army was to be maintained. This had a peacetime state – now organized by territory – which could be greatly expanded in wartime. Unofficially, the core peacetime units continued to be called *Kwarciani*, long after this reorganization.

During the 16th century the king maintained a **Court Army** (*wojsko nadworne*) separate from the state army. Hussars formed an important component, especially after 1576 when King Stefan Batory raised 1,000 court hussars, made up of 50- and 100-horse companies, and commanded by a court hetman (*Hetman nadworny*). The financing for this separate force disappeared in 1590 when the court treasury was separated from the state treasury. The king continued as titular *rotmistrz* of two hussar companies that bore his name (one each in Poland and Lithuania), but these were now on the state payroll.

Confusingly, the royal court continued to raise a hussar formation known as the **courtier company** (*choragiew dworzańska*), recruited from courtiers and fewer state functionaries, who each turned out a retinue for ceremonial occasions and accompanied the king to war. This exclusive company numbered 600 hussars during the 1609 Smolensk campaign, and 460 at Beresteczko (1651). It is the formation shown on the famous Stockholm roll (see Plates B and C).

BELOW **The armour display in c.1880–1900 at Podhorce Castle, now in Ukraine. Despite losses in World War I and the Russian Revolution, the collection in 1939 still contained 39 hussar breastplates and 65 lances, equipment that had been used in the 18th century by the hussar companies of hetmans of the Rzewuski family. The castle – one of Poland's great magnatial residences – is now an empty shell, and the contents are dispersed in Ukrainian, Polish and Russian collections.**

Many magnates kept **private armies** for protection and as ceremonial escorts. In peacetime these seldom numbered more than 100 dragoons and *haiduk* infantry, but several thousand more including superbly equipped hussars could be raised at short notice from client noblemen. Private units were often the first troops in theatre – as in the Swedish invasion of 1626 and the Ukranian Cossack Rebellion of 1648. In extended conflicts they were often taken on to the state payroll.

The ***Pospolite ruszenie*** or feudal levy of the nobles formed a last layer of defence for the realm and, in the 16th century, were still required to turn out as lance-armed knights. By the 17th century, most were equipped as *pancerny-kozak* cavalry. Some individuals equipped themselves as hussars, but few full units of hussars were fielded. From 1620 several provinces raised their own **district troops** (*wojsko powiatowe*) in place of noble levy. These were salaried professionals and often included hussars, but also proved reluctant to serve far from home.

EQUIPMENT

The state contributed very little to the costs of equipping hussars. The *towarzysz* himself covered the bulk of the expense as a career investment. In 1659 Poczobut-Odlanicki purchased a three-horse hussar *poczet* for 1,600 *zloty*, 'not overpaying, since I bought from my brother'. In terms of quarterly pay (at 51 *zloty* per horse) it would take him over two and a half years to recoup this sum. The *rotmistrz* also invested a substantial amount when raising a company, and paid for items such as lances, leopardskins and wings, as well as subsidizing his *towarzysze*. When setting up his own hussar company in 1621 the Lithuanian hetman Krzysztof Radziwill agreed to pay an extra 70 *zloty* per horse and to cover the cost of clothing the *pacholiks*. On rare occasions the 'start-up' costs were partly covered by the state; for example, in 1673 hussar pay was 200 *zloty* for the first quarter, falling to 51 *zloty* in subsequent quarters.

Both *towarzysz* and *rotmistrz* expected to recover some of their investment through pay and a share of war booty, but the biggest reward – especially for the *rotmistrz* – would be a lucrative state office granted (for life) by the king. Many *rotmistrze* were simultaneously granted the colonelcy of a western-style infantry regiment, the income of which helped offset the vast costs of maintaining a hussar company.

Armour

A new model of equipment was specified by King Stefan Batory in 'recruitment letters' issued for hussars of his Court Army in 1576–77. Their gear was to be in Hungarian style, the armour being 'properly made on the anvil from copper [i.e. brass] and iron'. In addition the hussar was to have:

helmet, iron [i.e. mail] sleeves, lance, sabre, the weapon or sword which they call a '*koncerz*', a firearm

BELOW **The *kapalin* helmet was worn by hussar retainers (rear-rankers) until the mid-17th century. Most are rather primitively made, with a faceted or grooved skull, articulated tail riveted to the brim, and a plume holder at rear. Almost identical helmets were worn by Swedish cavalry until c.1630, though theirs were more often blackened (as on this example) to prevent rust (See R. Brzezinski, *The Army of Gustavus Adolphus (2)*, Osprey MAA 262, pp. 44–5). (Fawley Court Museum, Henley-on-Thames, England)**

[*sclopetum*, pistol] carried on the saddle, feathers and other ornaments for splendour and to terrify the enemy according to the wish of each [captain]. (Pawinski, p. 54)

Batory was quite specific about the Hungarian style of armour, evidently intending it to replace the hotchpotch of western and eastern armour worn earlier. Its characteristic feature was the fully articulated, lobster-like *anima* breastplate that had originated in Italy, and was undoubtedly inspired by the *lorica segmentata* of Roman legionaries.

By 1600 breastplates began to take on a 'half-lobster' form, with only three or four bands or lames at the bottom. But it was only after the Turkish campaigns of 1620 and 1621 that the fashion for oriental weaponry really caught on in Poland, and the hussar armours of the style familiar to us today were produced from the 1630s – perversely, just as armour was being abandoned in western armies. The opulence increased further during the Golden Peace of 1638–48, and perhaps the most splendid turnout ever achieved by hussars was in 1648 at the outbreak of the Ukrainian Cossack Rebellion.

Hussar armour was spectacular to contemporaries, in part because it was burnished rather than blackened to prevent rust as in western armies. It was not particularly difficult or expensive to make, and both the steel surfaces and the brass fittings appear crude from close up. The sheer variety of surviving types is evidence of the large number of small workshops producing it. Given a supply of steel plate (produced in quantity by foundries in the Kielce region from about 1600) or a western armour of obsolete pattern, any small-town armourer could knock out a reasonably attractive suit of armour in hussar style. Towards the end of the 17th century a workshop in the Kraków region was supplying large consignments of hussar armours for captains throughout the Commonwealth, and it has been speculated that it produced many of the canonical hussar armours, especially those with Carpathian highland motifs, such as heart shapes, still seen in metalwork of the region today.

The hussar's helmet (*szyszak*, German *Zischägge*) for a long time followed Hungarian patterns. Like the armour, it began to evolve typically Polish features only from the 1620s or 1630s. These included bronze fittings and rivet heads finished as rosettes – symbols of the Virgin Mary – presumably invoking her protection.

The *pacholiks* in the rear ranks were given cheaper helmets such as the *kapalin* (Italian *capellina*), which had been popular in the 16th century. Most surviving examples are crude and apparently mass produced, though a few are better made, and Bielski in his *Kronika* of 1564 refers to hussars wearing 'gilded *kapalins* fitted with feathers in decorative clasps'. The last Polish images of *kapalins* date from the 1620s, but they may have persisted longer: many have been recovered from the banks of the Vistula in Warsaw, probably lost during the panic Polish retreat across the river at the battle of Warsaw in 1656; several of these are now in the city's Army Museum.

Batory's commissions required hussars to wear 'iron sleeves' (*manicis ferreis*). These have long been a puzzle, but they can probably be identified with the *zarekawie pancerzowe* – mail sleeves – listed in armoury inventories. A few early pictures show these worn with plate gauntlets.

ABOVE **Several suits of armour from the Podhorce collection are now on display at the arsenal in Lviv (Lwów), Ukraine. Although used in the 18th century, they are of the 'Older', i.e. early type (provisionally dated to 1640–75) with a characteristic ridge down the middle of each piece. The brass edging and heart-shaped aperture on the cheek-pieces are typical features of Polish armour. Note the single wing covered with plain leather.**

ABOVE AND OPPOSITE
Wing of the 'classic' style and a backplate of hussar armour. The wing has a wooden frame lined with velvet and reinforced with brass, and slots into a bracket on the backplate, which held it rigidly in place. Note, however, that the brass brackets on this armour (as on many others) seem to have been added later, indicating that backplate-mounted wings were a relatively late innovation. (Muzeum Wojska Polskiego)

Both mail sleeves and gauntlets were gradually replaced by oriental armguards known as *karwasze* (from Hungarian *kar* 'arm' and *vas* 'iron'). These appear in the inventories from about 1590, at first listed singly, suggesting they were originally worn on the bridle arm, though by 1630 they were common and worn in pairs.

In theory *pacholiks* received gear of inferior finish that nevertheless provided as good protection as that of the *towarzysz*. Craftsmen's price lists and contracts confirm that almost every item – from armour to lance – was made in a cheaper variant for the *pacholik*. However, not all *pacholiks* received such equipment. Pictures from the later 17th century often show rear-rankers dressed in fur caps and with little armour. Fredro in 1670 recommended reducing the size of *poczets* so the *towarzysz* could afford to equip his fewer retainers to a higher standard. Dalérac (the secretary to Sobieski's wife), writing in the 1690s, mentions that hussar '*pacolets*' had lance and helmet, but no cuirass, and instead wore only a '*juste-au-corps*' – meaning a long eastern coat.

In fact there was a general decline in the quantity of armour worn from the mid-17th century. Much equipment was lost in the Ukrainian Cossack Rebellion after 1648, and more was surrendered to or looted by the Swedes in 1655. When the Poles went on the counter-offensive in 1656, it proved impossible to supply all units with armour, and armoured hussars are rare in Swedish depictions of the conflict. Observers such as Raimondo Montecuccoli (who commanded an Imperial army in Poland in 1658) even described the contest as one between 'light-armed Poles and heavily armed Swedes'. During the 1660 Russian campaign the cavalryman Jakub Los mentions that only one hussar in ten wore armour. It was only in Sobieski's reign that the *husaria* regained its former splendour, initiating a second period of opulence that lasted until the late 18th century.

Swords

Many surviving Polish swords are gold-plated and encrusted with jewels; these were mostly fashion accessories – symbols of nobility, carried as part of everyday attire. Combat swords, described in the records as 'black', were plainer, with hand grips and scabbards of black leather.

The **sabre** (Polish *szabla*) evolved from Turkish and Hungarian prototypes. The 'Hungarian' style which became popular by the end of the 16th century had a particularly heavy blade and an open hilt, and was designed for delivering hacking blows at a gallop. A true mêlée sabre evolved only in the early decades of the 17th century: the blade became lighter, the hilt was closed to protect the hand, at first by means of a chainlet or an L-shaped bar, and finally a thumb-ring was added to help improve handling. The result was the 'Polish hussar sabre', one of the finest combat weapons of its day anywhere in Europe. The sabre had a number of sub-types, the best known of which is the *karabela*, with its bird-head-shaped pommel. This appeared toward the end of the 17th century, primarily as a dress sword, and was never specifically associated with the hussars.

Uniquely connected with the hussars was the **koncerz**, with its long (130–160cm) blade of triangular or square cross-section. The weapon is western in origin; its German name *Panzerstecher* ('mail-sticker') suggests its ability to pierce ring-mail – 'Panzer' in this period meant mail not plate armour. This name was often shortened to *Stecher*, hence *estoc* in French and *tuck* in English. The unwieldy *koncerz* was slung on the saddle, under the rider's thigh and (in the traditional view) almost parallel to the ground. However, during the filming of Jerzy Hoffman's *With Fire & Sword* (1998), re-enactors complained of the discomfort the weapon caused when slung this way. Examination of contemporary art shows the *koncerz* often hung at an angle of 45 degrees from the horizontal.

The **pallash** (Polish *palasz*, from Hungarian *pallos*) or broadsword, though outshone by the *koncerz*, appears in the sources far more frequently, suggesting it was more common. About 90–100cm in length, it had a straight blade, single- or double-edged, and a sabre-type hilt. Hungarian and German *pallashes* have straight blades; Polish ones are occasionally slightly curved. Confusingly, by the 18th-century Poles also used *palasz* to describe a type of close-hilted sabre.

Bows and firearms

While the mark of every Polish nobleman was his sabre, the specific badge of a *towarzysz*, notes Kitowicz, was his bow. This is why late 17th-century images occasionally show hussars carrying elegant bowcases, even though firearms made the bow as good as obsolete. Dalérac remarked that many Polish nobles carried bows as part of their everyday attire, but few were able to shoot them with any accuracy. As late as 1710 Karwicki noted that the habit of taking bows on campaign in the Great Northern War was making Polish horsemen a laughing stock among westerners: 'They should leave them at home', he comments.

The hussars were at first slow to adopt firearms. In 1525 each *poczet* was instructed to have a handgun (*rusznica*), and Hetman Jan Tarnowski's instructions of 1528 call this a long handgun (*pixidem manualem longam*). This was primarily intended for defence of the wagons and camp. Later instructions continue with this requirement for a long firearm, and various heavy-calibre wall-guns or hackbutts (*hakownice*) and muskets are often mentioned carried on the wagons.

The wheellock pistol came into widespread use as a cavalry weapon in the 1540s, but was taken up slowly in Poland, and into the 1560s no more than 30 per cent of hussars had them. Stefan Batory's 1576 commissions were instrumental in speeding up their adoption. Batory's official historian, Heidenstein, notes that at the initial muster for the Polock campaign (1579) cavalry fired their pistols as they defiladed before the king, to prove they owned functioning weapons. Contemporaries note that hussars carried one or two pistols, but until the 1630s the commissions indicate that only one was required. Western lancers at this time also carried only a single pistol, holstered on the left of the saddle pommel where it would not obstruct the lance. By the mid-17th century most hussars sported a pair of pistols, now much smaller and more reliable weapons equipped with French flintlocks.

The use of long-barrelled firearms by hussars is controversial. The historian Wimmer claims that by the mid-17th century the *pacholiks* in the rear ranks no longer had lances, and instead had a carbine known

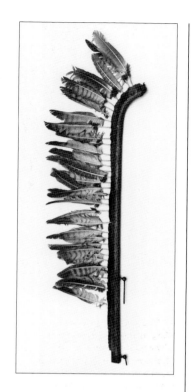

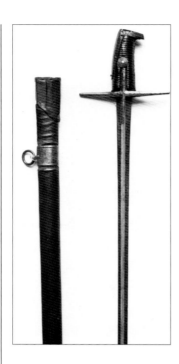

ABOVE *Koncerz* (tuck) with an early 17th-century 'Hungarian' open hilt, identical to that used on sabres. This is a 'black' or combat weapon, with corded hand grip and wooden scabbard both covered with black leather. Total length including hilt is 130cm. The blade is triangular in section. (Fawley Court Museum, Henley-on-Thames, England)

RIGHT **East European sword types from Marsigli's** *Stato militare dell Imperio Ottomano* **(1732): straight-edged** *pallash* **(E);** *koncerz* **with exceptionally long triangular or square blade (F), and various types of sabre (B, C, D). Traditionally, the word** *koncerz* **has been derived from** *khanjar/hanjar,* **the Arab dagger used by the Turks (A); but clearly the two weapons have little in common. More probably** *koncerz* **derives from a Slavic root:** *kończasty,* **'pointed'.**

as a *bandolet* after the leather shoulder belt on which it was slung. There is, in fact, little evidence that carbines were carried so early: in reality *pacholiks* continued to employ lances, but when sent on foraging duty or a raid would leave the lances behind and take up muskets from the wagons. Dalérac created a myth when he stated in his *Anecdotes de Pologne* (I, p. 22) that Hetman Jablonowski had in 1689 abolished the lance in favour of the musketoon (a heavy-calibre carbine). This was just a temporary measure when fighting the Tatars, against whom lances were of limited value. The latest research (Wagner, 2, pp. 142–3) shows that in the 1690s Jablonowski repeatedly instructed hussar *pacholiks* to have both lance and bandolet, so that they could be fielded with either as the tactical situation demanded. It is only in the 18th century that *pacholiks* permanently set aside the lance in favour of the bandolet or musketoon; *towarzysze* continued to employ the lance.

The *kopia* lance

The eastern lance or *kopia*, even more so than the wings, was the defining weapon of Polish hussars. Indeed, contemporaries often called them lancers. The *kopia*'s distinctive feature was its ball-shaped handguard, described by foreign visitors as an 'apple' (French *pomme*), but called a *galka*, 'knob' in modern Polish. A one-use weapon, the *kopia* was constructed of cheap, light wood such as pine or fir, the lighter the better. The shaft was hollowed to further reduce weight. Re-enactors have discovered that the best production method is to saw the raw wood billet lengthways, scoop out the interior and glue it together. Cardinal Valenti (1604) mentions that the two halves were 'conjoined with the most subtle sinews and threads of silk and the strongest glue, then painted in various colours, to mask the artifice'. The French engineer and traveller Guillaume le Vasseur de Beauplan mentions that the lance was hollowed only as far as the 'apple', the lower part being of solid wood. A veteran of the Balkan wars of *c*.1600, quoted by the historian Jähns (p. 1,005), stated that a '*Copi*' (probably of Hungarian hussars) of 14ft 6in weighed just $4\frac{1}{2}$lbs; whereas a 16ft 6in Dutch infantry pike weighed $5\frac{1}{2}$lbs.

The length of the *kopia* is given by contemporaries as anything from 13ft to 19ft (3.8–5.6m). The single, much-quoted reference by the military historian Bronislaw Gembarzewski (p. 33) to a 6.2m lance appears to be an error. His source, General-Major Kampenhausen, in 1737 refers to a lance of nearly 3 *sazhen* (arm-spans) length, but these are not 19th-century Russian *sazhen* of 2m plus, but rather old Polish ones of 6ft, giving a total length of 18ft (5.3m). The typical lance probably measured about 5m or 17 Polish feet, as recommended by

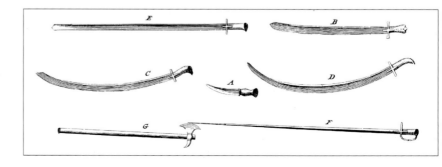

Fredro in 1670. (Polish writers quote length in ells, each of two feet, which measured 0.576–0.595m in different regions of Poland.) The few unbroken lances surviving in Poland are 4.80–4.90m long, but missing their heads; a single complete example measures 5.02m including its 18.5cm head.

Lance pennants were uniform within each company, and often followed the design of the company flag. Most were two-coloured, typically red/white, blue/white, yellow/black or white/black. Non-heraldic combinations such as blue/red and brick-red/black were also seen. At 3.5–4.0m long surviving pennants are huge. When the lance was lowered they would have touched the ground and become tangled in the horse's hooves. Though made of light silk they added to the lance's weight (especially when wet), and would become unmanageable in wind. Presumably shorter pennants were employed on campaign. Beauplan quotes a length of 'as much as 4 to 5 ells' (2.4–3.0m), Dalérac of 3 to 4 ells (1.8–2.4m), but pictorial sources often show pennants just 1–2m long. Clearly there was no standard size.

The replacement of lances during a campaign was always a problem and is mentioned after almost every pitched battle: 'We badly need hussar lances which none of us have, and it is difficult to obtain them in this region.' (Court Hetman Jan Zborowski to the king, three weeks after Lubieszów, 1577.) 'We broke all our lances: I doubt not that His Majesty will have the army re-equipped shortly.' (Crown Hetman Koniecpolski to the king, after Trzciana/Honigfelde, 1629.) The situation after defeats was no better – at Górzno (1629) the retreating hussars left the field strewn with unbroken lances. During the 'Deluge', supply was especially difficult. Prior to the recapture of Warsaw by Polish forces in early July 1656, according to the cavalryman Jakub Los, 'There were 9 Lithuanian hussar companies with lances; while in our [Crown] army not one had lances …' At Matwy (1666) during the Lubomirski rebellion, Los notes that in the rebel army only Lubomirski's own hussar company, in which he was personally serving, had lances.

Surviving contracts indicate that replacement lances were obtained in major cities near the theatre of war. In enemy territory improvisation was the only option. During the Russian campaign of 1660, the Polish cavalrymen Jan Chryzostom Pasek and Los note that several hussar companies used hop-poles with fire-hardened points, which they stained with vegetable dyes and surmounted with linen pennants.

The *kopia* continued in use until the end of the hussar. As late as 1739 the Lithuanian Field Hetman Michal Radziwill ordered 300 lances (enough to equip all the hussars of the Lithuanian army) from 'His Majesty's *kopia*-maker' Jakub Antonowicz in Lwów. These were to be 'painted crimson and black with gold feathers' – referring to the small painted feathers seen on the shafts of most surviving examples.

WINGS

No other element of hussar equipment is more misunderstood or obscured by legend than their wings. It is usually claimed that the first mention of Polish wings dates from 1553 when three riders appeared with 'silvered wings on their backs' at the wedding of King Zygmunt II

ABOVE **A hussar sabre with a fullered blade dated 1608 and marked with the initials and badge of Stanislaw Stadnicki, castellan of Przemysl (died 1611). The fully closed 'Polish' hilt was added to the blade in the later 17th century to improve protection for the hand, and incorporated a thumb-ring that allowed faster recovery of the weapon after a blow had been delivered. (Muzeum Wojska Polskiego, Warsaw, photo Miroslaw Ciunowicz)**

in Kraków. In fact, the passage in the royal secretary, Stanislaw Orzechowski's panegyric about the event was mistranslated from Latin in the 1800s; in reality these three riders were merely 'decorated with lofty feathers of birds' (*excelsis alitum pennis ornati*).

It is not until 1574 that clear references to wings appear, in descriptions of Henri de Valois' coronation in Kraków. For example, Gelée de Villemontée writes that the hussars have the 'custom of decorating themselves and their horses with large panaches, not of ostrich plumes like ours, but eagle's wings, striped with gold, which are so dense and so large in extent that they are made expressly for masquerades, or to frighten people.' Other descriptions of the coronation mention whole companies wearing wings attached to their shields and the manes of their horses.

By 1575 it is clear that some of these wings were worn on the back, but the overall impression is that all these early wings are of the same 'naturalistic' type worn by Serbian and Bosnian *deli* and *grenzer* scouts. When Batory standardized the hussars in 1576 he abolished shields – so removing one of the favourite locations for tacking these early wings. But, as mentioned earlier, the use of 'featherware' was a requirement of his recruitment letters. One intriguing possibility is that the shields were briefly replaced by wooden imitation wings, worn on the rider's arm, as in the Stuttgart carousel of 1616 (see picture on this page).

By the 1590s, a new site for the wing had been found at the back of the saddle – on the left side where a single wing would not interfere with the lance. These early wings were made of a simple row of feathers inserted into a straight batten. By 1600 clear images of these saddle-mounted wings, occasionally worn in pairs, become so plentiful that there can be no doubt that this was the main type worn until at least the 1650s.

What then of the 'classical' frame wings worn on the back? The French diplomat Charles Ogier (1635) may be the first to mention these. He states that the hussars' dress is splendid, 'but it is difficult not to laugh at the sight of the long wings attached at their backs, which, they claim, scare the enemy horses and throw the enemy into retreat'. Unfortunately, the original Latin is too vague to be sure these are not saddle-mounted wings. The first reliable illustration of a back-mounted 'frame' wing is that worn by Colonel Szczodrowski at Paris in 1645 (see pictures on p. 22).

During the crisis of the 1650s and 1660s wings appear to have fallen out of use. Lubomirski's Italian secretary Cefali (1665) wrote that the hussars 'had the custom of attaching huge vulture wings at their backs, which at the gallop made a great rustling noise; but now hardly anyone uses them.' Sobieski's reign saw a

BELOW **Hussars on parade during the 'carousel' held in Stuttgart to mark the baptism in 1616 of Friedrich, son of the Duke of Württemberg. The riders portrayed the Hungarian knight 'Lasla Janush' and his six sons. The wings, which are attached to the rider's arm, are described in accompanying text as 'wing-shields'. Although the engraver Matthaeus Merian may be in error, these may represent a 'missing link' in the evolution of the wing.**

revival of the hussars, and wings evidently came back into fashion. Descriptions by authors such as Dalérac and a few rare pictures suggest these wings were now mainly back-mounted. For a detailed description of the classic forward-curved wings we must, however, wait until the 18th century, and the ever-valuable Kitowicz:

> Hussar troopers had screwed to the rear of their armour a piece of wood reaching from the belt, high above the head, and curving over the head; inserted into this from one end to the other were a row of feathers painted in various colours, looking like a laurel or palm branch which made a strangely pretty sight, though not all companies used such laurel branches.

The conservative Lithuanians lagged behind, and Kitowicz notes that they continued to wear the old style saddle-mounted wings: 'the Lithuanian hussars … after mounting the horse, fastened to the left side a huge wing made of ostrich feathers, which covered the whole side of the horse and the rider's leg to his ankles.'

What were the wings for?

The consensus today is that wings were purely a parade adornment, yet there is evidence that they were taken on campaign. In 1609 a Kraków craftsmen commented that 150 *zloty* was a small sum for the 32 eagle's wings he had manufactured 'which each (hussar) for greater adornment is *required* to wear in pairs on the *march*', though he claimed he would have received more for them 'in time of need, such as a wedding or a triumph'.

During the Vienna campaign of 1683, the monk Brulig mentions Polish hussars 'each with two eagle wings … more parading than marching' past his monastery 15km south of Brno in Moravia. So there can be no doubt that wings – like the hussar's elegant silk clothing and parade horse harness – were indeed worn on campaign. Such finery, states Kitowicz, was not worn on a daily basis, as it would quickly wear out, but was reserved for special occasions. In poor weather or difficult terrain (such as woods) wings would have been left on the wagons.

But were wings worn in battle? They are often shown in contemporary battle paintings, but these were seldom painted by eyewitnesses. Frustratingly, no one has yet found a single reliable, non-poetic eyewitness to confirm that wings were routinely worn in battle.

Did the wings make a noise during the charge? The short answer is no. This idea goes back to two foreign visitors – Cefali (1665) and Dalérac (1680s) – neither of whom saw any action. There are also (poetic) references to wings on parade making a rustling noise, but these probably refer to a sort of buzzing sound in a strong wind. The

BELOW **One of the four contemporary images (see also following pages) of the same winged hussar during the Polish embassy to Paris in 1645. Here he is falsely identifed as 'Bilinski grand equerry', from a contemporary Parisian engraving by Campion. Here the hussar wing is shown high on the back, giving the impression, as Kitowicz later noted, of a palm branch.**

ABOVE LEFT **Polish rider with a back-mounted wing, from Stefano Della Bella's sketch of the 1645 ceremonial entry into Paris of a Polish delegation to fetch the future queen of Poland, Marie-Louise de Gonzaga. The rider is identified as 'Mr Szcodroski' – actually, Colonel Krzysztof Szczodrowski, who led the ambassador's 'honour guard of gentlemen', and had earlier recruited Polish cavalry for Wallenstein in 1633. (M. Paszkiewicz, *Stefano della Bella: 'Wjazd wspanialy poslów polskich do Paryza A.D. 1645'*, London 1956)**

ABOVE RIGHT **Colonel Szczodrowski engraved by Della Bella from his earlier sketch. In the background the rider is shown in different poses, even leaning forward, the wing attached directly to his back. This is the first, indeed only, clear image of a back-mounted frame wing during the 17th century, and significantly it is worn without armour. Note also the servant on the right.**

idea that wings made a noise loud enough to scare the enemy over the terrific din of a cavalry charge is patently absurd. During the filming of Jerzy Hoffman's epic *With Fire & Sword* near Poznan in May 1998, the author personally witnessed repeated charges of 50 winged hussars and not a murmur came from the wings.

There have been several other theories on the purpose of wings. In his account of a visit to Poland in 1588, the papal legate Ippolito Aldobrandini stated that as well as scaring enemy horses, the wings protected against sword cuts. More recently T. Tilinger in 1949 saw wings as a defence against Tatar lassoes, imagining their original form was two vertical rails attached to the armour back plate, which gradually acquired feathers as decoration. Jerzy Teodorczyk in the 1970s suggested wings might be a souvenir – a sort of campaign medal – for units that had served in the Turkish wars.

Most such theories fall foul of chronology. In the mid-16th century, before they appeared in Poland, wings were worn (and their function therefore established) by Balkan *deli* horsemen. In Ottoman miniatures, *delis* often wear their wings in action. It is little known that the Poles had their own version of the *deli* – the *elear*. Like *delis*, *elears* were reckless daredevils, *enfants perdus*, whose function was to advance ahead of the main army and open the battle by disrupting the enemy, either by provoking him to charge first or by disordering his formation with a sacrificial charge. Their name derives either from Hungarian *elöljaro* – 'riding foremost' or from Latin *eligeri* – 'chosen men' (see Plate E3).

Ad hoc units of *elears*, selected four from each hussar company and numbering about 100 men in total, played a prominent role at Pitschen (1588), Bucou (1600 – where they almost won the battle by themselves), Kokenhusen (1601) and Guzów (1607). With the increasing lethality of firearms their role was replaced in the 1620s by skirmishing light horse. However, writing in the 1680s after a visit to the Polish court, many decades after *elears* had fallen out of use, the French poet Regnard seems to have been informed of their original battlefield role:

> The servants of the men [hussars] precede the squadron on horseback, with a lance in their hand; and it is very singular that these people have wings attached to their backs: they rush occasionally into the midst of their enemies, and frighten their horses, who are unaccustomed to such visions, and make way for their masters, who closely follow them.

The one element common in nearly all the accounts is that the hussar's wings were intended to frighten the enemy. They did this not by any alleged whistling sounds but by visual impact.

ABOVE **Another image of the Polish hussar in Paris, again identified as 'Bilinski, equerry of the Polish ambassador'. Detail of a print of the 'Magnificent Entry' by Jean Boisseau, published in Paris in 1645. As often happens, the artist has only vaguely remembered the hussar wing and has 'corrected' it to a more natural shape.**

Horses are wary of unfamiliar sights, and one or two flustered horses might be enough to disrupt an entire enemy formation. Indeed the whole gear of the hussar – leopardskin, wings, fluttering pennants and dazzling armour – was designed to intimidate and overawe the enemy, much like the guardsman's bearskin hat in later centuries. The wings and fur evoked a primitive visceral fear of predatory animals. This certainly is the impression conveyed by witnesses such as Heinrich Wolf of Zurich, who at Batory's coronation in 1576 noted that the thousands of Polish horsemen were 'so well covered with the pelts of sables, lynxes and bears, that one might think it was an army not of people but of wild animals, riding winged pegasuses [the winged horse of legend] in place of horses.'

Ultimately, the wings lost their original purpose and began to serve as a sort of branch-of-service badge for the hussars. By the late 17th century feathers were even being painted on hussar lances. In a ceremony of 1646 we hear of 'feathered units' as a synonym for hussars.

CLOTHING

Hungarian styles of male costume arrived in Poland in the early 16th century; their adoption was intimately linked with the growing importance of hussars in the army. Indeed, for decades the terms 'Hungarian' and 'hussar' were interchangeable. At first Polish garments differed little from their Hungarian prototypes, though skirts grew longer and fabrics thicker in the cooler Polish climate. By the 17th century, however, many new garments in Tatar, Russian and Turkish cut were appearing in Poland, and fashions and terminology changed rapidly.

For most of our period, the hussar *towarzysz* did not wear uniform clothing, but dressed as well as he could afford. The modern stereotype is that his garments were red. This was the colour of the highest echelons of the nobility, the *karmazyni* or 'carmines' whose dazzling robes were coloured with an expensive dyestuff – Polish kermes, extracted from the tiny *Porphyrophora polonica* insect (native to eastern Europe), which produced a spectacular scarlet dye.

A cheaper blue colour was far more common among the middling nobles, as the traveller Ulrich von Werdum commented in the 1670s: 'The outer garments of the ordinary Polish nobles are blue, while lords and magnates, as well as the richest merchants, wear other colours.' Evidence from probate inventories indicates that even poorer nobles often owned garments in a variety of colours whose names would not shame a modern interior decorator: papagay (parrot green), sulphur, coral, soot, pepper, cinnamon, clove (pink), to mention only a few.

The more splendid garments were reserved for parades and 'off-duty' activities, when hussars paid visits to each other's tents, and to the nearby homes of family and friends. On extended campaigns practicality took over. The cleric and reformer Szymon Starowolski (1628, pp. 37–9) notes that on parade, hussars wore silk, gold and gems, but on campaign 'everyone makes use of cheaper materials'.

Hussars in battle paintings are depicted in a wide range of colours. Even so, uniforms – in the sense of clothing of a standard colour and cut – were far more common than often believed, especially in companies raised by wealthy magnates. Such commanders spared no expense to ensure their companies looked their best; indeed on state occasions, such as royal weddings, the majority of hussar units seem to have worn 'uniform' clothing.

Even in wartime there was plenty of uniformity among hussar *pacholiks* (retainers). These impoverished men seldom enlisted with their own presentable clothing, and since their appearance reflected on the unit as a whole, clothing them was a priority. When a company was first raised, the *rotmistrz* often agreed to pay for clothing the retainers (see for example the 1621 agreement for Krzysztof Radziwill's hussars mentioned above). Replacement clothing was obtained fairly regularly. In 1618 the memoirist Maskiewicz (then *porucznik* of Count Janusz Porycki's hussar company) records (p. 212) how he travelled to Wilno 'to procure livery [*barwa*] for the "*czeladz*" [presumably his retainers]'. In 1661 Poczobut-Odlanicki (p. 150), then a hussar *towarzysz*, also comments that he had 'procured livery for the *czeladz*' as if this were a routine chore. Although writing in the late 18th century, Kitowicz mentions that retainers 'had since long long ago' been issued with uniforms. Such clothing was regarded as an issued item like weapons and armour: the Articles of War forbade retainers from lending out, pawning, selling or, heaven forbid, gambling them away, under the severest penalties.

BELOW **Polish *elear* scout in 1627–28, from the travel diary of the Dutch diplomat, Abraham Booth, *Journael van de Legatie* (Amsterdam 1632). He has little armour, and carries a bow and quiver and a shield with cross emblem. His wings are attached high on the shoulders and are of the same 'naturalistic' type worn in the 16th century by the Ottoman *deli*.**

Leopardskins and capes

One of the more exotic elements of hussar attire was the leopardskin. In written accounts tiger and panther skins are mentioned almost as often, but since few Europeans had seen such animals the terms were largely interchangeable. It seems that a feline pelt with spots was what was required, and if a skin did not have spots, they would be stained on.

The light pelts depicted on the Stockholm roll may well be snow leopards – once quite common in the Caucasus and Central Asia. On some pictures the leopard's head is still attached to the skin, and the chronicler Rudawski mentions Poles wearing 'lions with open jaws' at the start of the Ukranian Cossack Rebellion in 1648. On many pictures the skins look more like rectangular capes, presumably sewn together from smaller feline pelts, such as lynxes. Undoubtedly influenced by hussar fashion, spotted lynx-fur collars were all the rage on civilian garments.

In view of their cost, leopardskins were often supplied by the *rotmistrz*, or in the case of royal hussar companies, by the king himself. Many contemporaries mention that instead of leopardskins hussar *pacholiks* wore wolfskins. Again, these were usually provided by the *rotmistrz*. In 1621 the *porucznik* of Hetman Krzysztof Radziwill's hussars wrote that he had only been able to obtain '47 wolf capes [*delur wilczych*]' (Wisner, III, p. 93). This is further evidence of the re-cutting of skins in garment shape.

Several Polish battle paintings show hussars not in leopardskins, but in dazzling striped capes reminiscent of Navajo blankets. Before the advent of colour photography few Polish authorities had seen how spectacular these capes could be and called them *kilims* after a type of Turkish rug. The contemporary term was *welens*, from the Turkish *velense* or *velençe*, a shaggy rectangular blanket with a long nap on one side often used as a horse covering, named according to the historian Tezcan, after the Spanish city of Valencia, the original home of the tailors who produced them.

Surviving *welense* in Istanbul are white with garish striped patterns. Polish *welense* were made of colourful fine-quality woollen cloth, although plain *welense* for *pacholiks* are listed among the products of Armenian craftsmen in a statute of 1650 (VL 4, f.358). Striped *welense* are often mentioned in the early 17th century. For example at King Wladyslaw IV's 1637 wedding, 15 hussars of a *poczet* raised by the starosta of Miedzyrzec for the Courtier Company wore 'scarlet *welense* with stripes of yellow satin'.

To be fair to earlier historians, similar capes were later called *kilims*. During the 1658 Denmark campaign Pasek stated that the red *kilims* of the retainers of the Voivode of Sandomierz's hussar company led to them being known as gypsies. Gypsy clothing at this time was often striped, which may explain the allusion.

The different animal pelts and capes worn by hussar officers, *towarzysze* and retainers caused much confusion among western observers, leading Sobieski's Irish physician Bernard Connor, for example, to imagine he was looking at three entirely different classes of cavalry.

HORSES

'A Pole without a horse is like a body
without a soul.'
(Old Ruthenian saying)

The Polish nobility were accomplished horsemen and loved their horses. Especially valued were oriental breeds with Arab blood, known generally as 'Turks'. The royal stud at Knyszyn near Bialystok was one of the first in Christian Europe to breed these, and in 1565 stabled 3,000 horses of various breeds.

Hussar horses were perhaps not the destriers of western chivalry, but nor were they small animals. In 1568 the papal nuncio Ruggieri noted that Polish steeds were 'quite large … slower in running than Turkish horses, albeit stronger and prettier than them'. However, he believed Lithuanian horses were 'much smaller and weaker than Polish ones'.

Until 1563 company registers specified the grade of horse owned by every cavalryman. While hussar horses were valued for compensation at 7–15 *zloty*, 'Turks' were valued at 30 *zloty* (Bielski, *Sprawa rycerska*, 1569). The desirability of oriental horses led Polish breeders to introduce Arab blood into existing stocks. In the 1950s the hippologist Witold Pruski

BELOW **Krzysztof Radziwill (1585–1640), commander (hetman) of the Lithuanian army in campaigns against Sweden in the 1610s and 1620s. Like many hussars his 'leopardskin' is actually a thick cape made from two different furs. The armour is an example of the huge variety of suits worn by hussars; the fan-like arrangement of plates covering the armpit is thought to be a Swiss innovation. (Engraving of 1639 by W.J. Delff of a painting by M. Mierevelt)**

noticed two intriguing trends. Heavy western breeds, generally termed *fryz* (Frisian), tend to deteriorate in the Polish climate over a few generations. Arabs, by contrast, put on height and mass, without losing any of their good looks and quality, and often become much stronger and faster. It would seem that in the 17th century Polish breeders balanced these divergent tendencies to produce a superb-looking animal that was strong, solid and fast. It was the perfect cavalry horse, and many thousands were supplied to western armies, especially during the Thirty Years War (1618–48), despite repeated attempts (for example in 1620 – VL 3 f.374) to ban their export.

After his experience in Poland in the 1710s Marshal Maurice de Saxe (in his famous *Reveries*) considered 15 hands 2 inches the minimum for mounting the armoured lancers, which he hoped to reintroduce in western armies. This appears to be the size for which much surviving hussar horse furniture was made.

Horses represented the single largest expense of raising hussars. In 1633 the horses of Radziwill's Lithuanian hussar company were assessed to be worth 120–300 *zloty* each (Wisner, III, p. 87). In the same year the last will of a Polish hussar, Jan Zabokrzycki, valued the three horses of his *poczet* at 220, 120 and 100 *zloty* (J. Syganski, *Z zycia szlachty sandeckiej*, 1910, p. 101). Another reliable figure is given by Poczobut-Odlanicki, who in 1659 paid 300 *zloty* compensation for the dapple-grey horse of a fellow *towarzysz* that he shot accidentally, although the owner claimed it was worth 600. So, averaged over the *poczet*, a hussar's horse represented about a year's salary.

Most hussar *towarzysze* took additional horses on campaign to spare their main mount, plus draught horses for the wagons: army regulations strictly banned the harnessing of war horses to pull these. There were always two or three times as many horses with each *poczet* as listed on the company register.

TRAINING

Every prospective *towarzysz* was able from a young age to ride and to wield a sabre, both skills he learned at home. The system of training that produced the medieval knight survived in Poland, though it was fast disappearing, much lamented by Szymon Starowolski.

Starowolski harked back fondly to the knightly training he had witnessed in his youth. He wrote that 'on every holy-day' young noblemen would engage in a variety of 'chivalric' sports on their estates. 'Running at the ring' was a particular favourite – catching with the lance a small ring suspended from a wooden framework. Experienced lancers were able to pick up a piece of paper or a *magierka* cap from the ground. Other displays of skill included mounting a horse

LEFT 'The Polish horse', an engraving by J.E. Ridinger, from c.1725–50. There was no single breed of 'Polish horse' in this period, but many regional varieties with shared characteristics. Hussar horses were selected from the best available and were essentially of western type with a small admixture of Arab blood. It is thought that they most resembled the modern Wielkopolski breed, unlike this animal, which has the small head of an Arab.

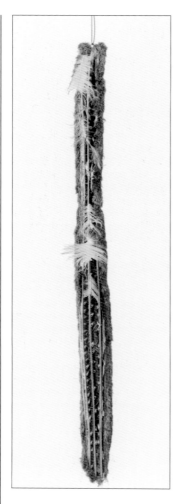

ABOVE AND OPPOSITE **The 'Skokloster' wing is the only surviving Polish wing that can be dated with confidence. It appears in the earliest (1710) inventory of the armoury at Skokloster near Uppsala, Sweden, formed by Carl Gustav Wrangel (died 1676), and was almost certainly taken in Poland in 1655–56. The single wing measures 110cm and is constructed of three battens of soft wood, to which white ostrich feathers are wired and glued. Voids are filled with flax-like fibres. The outer surface is covered with linen fabric glued in place, over which is a layer of fringed red velvet. Two holes, at 11cm and 46cm from the base, are the only means of fastening. (With thanks to Bengt Kylsberg)**

without touching the bow of the saddle, and lifting three lances together by their heads.

More reckless individuals risked their lives in the dangerous 'hussar' jousts with sharp lances, which took place *al campo aperto* – in the open field – without a barrier to prevent collisions. One of the last major hussar tournaments followed the royal wedding of 1605, though the Italian Antonino Ansalone in his *Il cavaliere* of 1629 commented that Poles continued to be addicted to this exceptionally hazardous form of jousting – which he believed originated in Poland – not as a sport, but as 'an excuse to pointlessly throw their lives away'.

By the 1640s, however, Starowolski was complaining that the youth were growing soft. The reality was that most young noblemen had long since learnt the bulk of their military skills only after entering service. Recruitment letters required that the *rotmistrz*, when forming his company, was to base it around a core of veteran *towarzysze*. The 1609 Articles of War – the main regulations for the Crown Army – encouraged special attention be given to training the 'inexperienced *towarzysze* and *pacholiks*', and also encouraged the *rotmistrz* to personally drill his entire company in formation as a way to 'more easily discern deficiencies in its horses and equipment' (*WZ* 5, p. 129).

Traditionally it is thought that hussars gradually worked their way up the hierarchy of the *towarzysz* system, which is often compared to a medieval guild, with apprentices and masters. It is said that a young hussar started as a servant, then served as a *pacholik*, before finally raising a *poczet* of his own. But this is taking the analogy too far. It is unlikely that any nobleman would have started off as a lowly camp servant, keeping company with peasants. Few diarists give details of their earliest years of service, but Poczobut-Odlanicki, for example, served on his first campaign aged 16 or 17, apparently as a *pacholik* while learning his craft.

The most important skill for a hussar to master was handling the lance while struggling to control his powerful mount. In 1676 Sobieski commented that the hussar horse required a severe bridle with a curb bit (*munsztuk*), 'since it is difficult to use the second [i.e. lance] hand' (*WZ* 6, p. 78). In effect the mount largely had to be steered with leg movements alone. One exercise was regarded by equestrian writers such as Pieniazek (1607) as specific to the hussars. This involved galloping along a narrow marked track, and then turning within 3m circles at either end without the horse's hooves stepping out. This drill took several months to perform with confidence.

Horses and riders were accustomed to charging in formation in an exercise that altered little from the 16th to 18th centuries. The hussars were divided into two groups facing each other. The approach began, lances were lowered and the two formations charged each other at full tilt, passing through gaps left between them: 'It will appear when looking from afar as if the formations are fighting', commented Bielski in 1569. Soon after the battle of Vienna in 1683, Sobieski arranged a demonstration at the German emperor's request, apparently without prior rehearsal. According to the writer Dyakowski (p. 73), Sobieski had 24 hussars divide into two groups, which charged each other, aiming their lances at the riders' breasts, but suddenly pulled them upright before impact, to the astonishment of the German observers.

The best 'school' of war was, of course, active service, especially among the *Kwarciani* regulars, who were on permanent station in the Ukraine on year-round alert for Tatar raids and unrest among the Ukrainian Cossacks. Des Noyers considered the *Kwarciani* 'the elite of the army, like the Praetorians of Rome'. Attempts were made to circulate novice hussars through the *Kwarciani* to create a reservoir of skilled men who could be called up in wartime. But the massacres of the *Kwarciani* at Zolte Wody and Korsun in 1648, and again at Batoh in 1652, had a far greater effect than the immediate loss of manpower – like the Katyn massacre of 1940, they deprived the army of its veteran cadre for training. The effects were to be felt in a lack of professionalism exhibited by Polish troops in the later 17th century.

ON CAMPAIGN

Most major campaigns conducted by the Polish army followed a time-worn schedule. By the time the rickety machinery of state had voted funds to raise troops, and these had gathered at the allotted concentration point from the various provinces of Poland, a campaign rarely got under way before July. This meant that against Russia or Turkey decisive actions often took place in the autumn, and campaigning continued until after the first snows.

After mustering at the concentration point, the army's cavalry was divided into *pulks* (formations intermediate between modern regiments and divisions) and was reviewed in full battle order by the king or hetman. Behind the pomp was the practical need for each soldier to learn how his company slotted into larger tactical formations, and for commanders to acquaint themselves with the chain of command. Each *pulk* then marched off, often on a separate route to lessen the burden on the Commonwealth's rather inadequate roads.

Baggage and logistics

Polish armies on the march seemed chaotic to foreigners. Unlike western armies where the wagons were collected into a baggage train, each Polish company marched with its own wagons. Starowolski describes the 'tail' of just one small hussar company in his 'True knight' (*Prawy Rycerz*) of 1648:

> Last year near the town of Rzeszów I came across a company of only 60 hussars, and counted 225 wagons, of which nearly half were four- and six-horse vehicles, not to mention the loose horses, women and children on foot who were countless.

The vast numbers of wagons and servants that accompanied every company were an effect of the Polish system of recruitment based around the *poczet*, which acted as an independent economic community. Another factor was the low population density in the Commonwealth, which made it difficult to provision any sizeable force from local supplies. Ultimately the *towarzysz* was responsible for the feeding of his

OPPOSITE **Encampment for a hussar company from the 1659 manuscript of engineer Naronowicz-Naronski's *Military architecture*. At top, with the largest area, are the quarters of the *rotmistrz* (key): a. – *rotmistrz's* tent (*szopa* – a word that now means hut); b. – tent; c. – tent (*kotarka*) lined with cloth or rugs for sleeping; d. – accommodation for youths and pages; e. – accommodation for *czeladz*; f. – oven with chimney; g. – stable for 16 horses; h. – kitchen and food tent; i. – food store; k. – tent for horse fodder; l. – wagons; m. – spare tent; n. – latrine. Below this are the quarters of the *porucznik* (lieutenant) with stabling for 8–10 horses; then the standard-bearer with seven or eight horses, while each *towarzysz* has space for six or seven horses.**

poczet, and did so largely out of the stores stowed on his wagons. This was an advantage when it came to travelling through devastated regions or over the empty Ukrainian steppe, giving a high degree of self-sufficiency at minimal cost to the state.

The *rotmistrz*'s recruitment letter often stated in detail the items every *poczet* was expected to have in its wagons, from tents of various kinds, down to axes and shovels for building entrenchments and latrines. A list of property lost at Zbaraz (1649) by Jakub Michalowski, *Chorazy* (standard-bearer) of the Royal Courtier Company of Hussars, gives some idea of the variety of wagons that a single *poczet* might own:

2 baggage wagons covered with red cloth [tilts] each with 6 horses,
A baggage wagon covered with leather with 4 horses,
A small wagon with a pair of horses,
A plain wagon with 4 horses,
A *teleszka* (Russian peasant carriage) with one horse,
An ox cart with victuals and with 5 oxen.
(M. Nagielski, *Relacje wojenne … 1648–1651*, Warsaw 1999, p. 358)

Many of the victuals carried on the wagons would be familiar to modern Poles, and included buckwheat (*kasza*), peas, dried bread (*suchary*), smoked meats, and hard cheeses of a type still made today in the Carpathian region.

One commodity considered indispensable was lard – the comic poem 'Albertus goes to war' (*Wyprawa Plebanska*, 1590) notes that besides its mundane culinary uses, lard could be used to prevent rust on armour, lubricate sword scabbards and soften leatherware; 'smear it on your lance just before action, and it will glisten like freshly painted.' It could even be used to treat wounds to horses.

Wagons were progressively consumed during the campaign. According to the military engineer Dupont (p. 241): 'When a wagon is empty it is burned; the oxen are killed and the meat is distributed as rations. In this manner the army disposes unconsciously of the great number of wagons which follow it at the start of a campaign.'

When the wagons were empty, provisioning fell, in theory, on sutlers who accompanied the army and on local traders. But the mere presence of an army often caused food prices to double or treble. Inevitably troops resented the price hikes that they could not afford and began scavenging for supplies, which quickly degenerated into robbery and worse. Contemporaries identified the inadequacy in logistics as the root of all indiscipline in the Polish army, and though some remedies were attempted – such as setting up magazines along march routes – the state treasury was too depleted to maintain them.

Camp life

Once the camp was set up, and each *poczet* was lodged in its tents, the *towarzysz* settled down to a boisterous social life. A *towarzysz* rarely mixed with his own retainers and servants; rather he kept company with other *towarzysze* and his *rotmistrz* and, to the amazement of foreigners, he often dined at the hetman's table. Such gatherings were inevitably lubricated by alcohol. Vodka, being easy to transport or to distil with rudimentary apparatus, became the drink of the military, and hussars, like the 'idle rich' of every age, were notorious for their drinking. The satirist and soldier Waclaw Potocki (1621–96) describes a Frenchman entering a Polish bar to see a filthy-drunk hussar *towarzysz* 'vomiting *bigos* (cabbage stew) onto a table from his mouth and nose …' 'This is not like Paris', huffs the Frenchman. 'Welcome to Poland', comments Potocki.

All too often drinking binges left troops and commanders incapacitated in their tents, bringing campaigning to a halt. Better commanders would be able to enforce discipline in the camp, filling vacant time with training and religious devotions.

The *towarzysz*, as a gentleman, was excused most of the menial duties of camp life. Some of these fell on his *pacholiks*, unfortunately shadowy figures who rarely wrote diaries. The many criminal cases that resulted from the passing of almost every Polish army suggest they were often up to no good, drinking like the *towarzysze*, and then getting into vicious fights.

Below the *pacholiks* were the camp servants – the dogsbodies of the unit. A good idea of the lot of a camp servant is seen in Piotr Baryka's 1637 poem *Z chlopa król (A peasant made king)*:

You're never free day or night:
In the morning it's harness my horse, brush my coat,
If you don't please him, he thumps you.
Then it's muck out the stables, …
And as for eating – Dear God, what could be worse!
You watch like a puppy for something to drip from his moustache. …
Indeed, dogs often eat better than hussar servants. …
And when they get drunk, oh, pity the poor servant …
It's jump over this bared sword, or hold up this coin,
which he then shoots from your fingers.

Army regulations required some *towarzysze* always to be present in camp to maintain order among the servants. Such duties were performed in rotation, so that all *towarzysze* gradually acquired command experience. Each company was responsible for its own fodder, and obtaining this was a key chore of the servants, who would leave camp to exercise and water the horses and take the opportunity to scour the neighbouring countryside ruthlessly for anything edible.

More aggressive foraging missions were delegated to the *pacholiks* supervised by a handful of *towarzysze*. For these, the cavalry left behind the wagons and heavier equipment – often including the hussars' lances – and travelled in *komunik* (from Ruthenian *komon* 'horse') – meaning with only what their horses could carry. The memorist Samuel Maskiewicz (pp. 124–5) describes one such raid during the Smolensk campaign of 1610. In all 1,800 *pacholiks* were drawn out from the army,

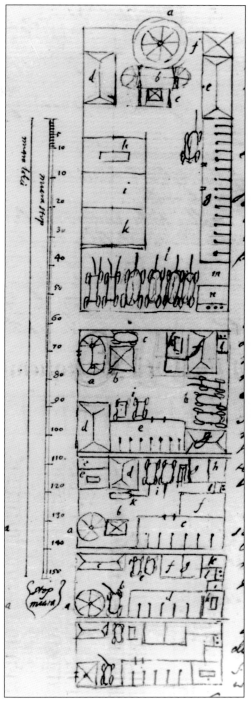

and attached to them 'to ensure better discipline were two *towarzysze* from each company'. This ad hoc force not only found food, but also captured and thoroughly looted the Russian town of Roslav, 110km south-east of Smolensk.

Siege warfare, involving long months holed up in camp, rather than sweeping charges, was the reality of most campaign life. Hussars were not expected to do manual labour, but would often stand mounted in formation and under fire to provide cover while infantry and dragoons dug entrenchments. When defending a *tabor* or wagon-fort, the infantry and camp servants would be left to hold the perimeter, while the hussars were preserved as a mounted reserve, ready to sally out if the attackers slipped their guard.

In protracted sieges, the hussar *pacholiks* took their turn manning the ramparts, and often participated in storming operations, with one or two *towarzysze* to command them. The participation of *towarzysze* in such dangerous operations was entirely voluntary. Nevertheless, large numbers of *towarzysze* often took part, as at Pskov (1581) and Pernau (1609). At Smolensk in August 1610, however, they initially refused to assist in a storming operation, because they had been ordered to the task, rather than requested to it.

With the increasing use of field works in warfare against the Swedes and Turks, and of wooden field obstacles by the Russians, even field battles often resembled sieges. At Lojów in 1649, the hussar *towarzysze* dismounted to lead the final victorious assault against the Ukranian Cossack wagon-fort.

Hussar *towarzysz*, 1590s

A

Company of Courtiers (*Choragiew Dworzañska*), 1605

1

B

2

3*

4

5*

Company of Courtiers (continued)

1

2

3*

4*

6

7*

5

c

A Hussar *poczet* in camp, 1620s/30s

D

The evolution of hussar wings

E

Hussar *towarzysz*, c.1680s

F

The charge of Prince Alexander Sobieski's company at Vienna, 1683

G

The universal soldier?

Starowolski (1648) liked to think of the hussar as the universal soldier: 'When necessary, he cast aside the lance to become a *Reiter* [German-style horseman] with gun and *pallash*; taking off his armour he became a *kozak* horseman; and if the king or hetman only asked it, he was an infantryman in armour.' This is all stirring rhetoric, as we would expect of a patriotic cleric, but how much truth is there in it?

One of the chief criticisms of hussars cited by contemporaries was that they were of little use for anything but pitched battles. They could not be employed on everyday campaign duties as the condition of their horses would quickly deteriorate. Maurice de Saxe became a great fan of the heavy lancer after extensive service in Poland in the 1710s. On Polish-style lancers he later wrote: 'one should regard them like the heavy artillery, which … for most of the time is little more than a burden on the baggage train.'

Another admirer of the Polish hussar was General-Major J.J. Kampenhausen (*c.*1680–1742), a Baltic German who served widely in the Great Northern War. In his *Chwala i Apologia Kopii i Pik (Praise and apology for the lance and pike)*, Kalisz 1737, he answered criticism of the lancer: 'The Poles have a saying – cheap meat is eaten by dogs.' Lancers may be expensive he says, but you get what you pay for. 'Good for only one day of battle?' Kampenhausen continues, 'Yes, but what a day – the day of decision!'

BATTLE FORMATIONS

Throughout the 16th century the main tactical formation of Polish cavalry was the **huf** (from Middle High German *Hufe*, modern German *Haufen*, 'battle-formation'). This was made up of several companies, grouped apparently as a single contiguous body. The *huf* was the chief operating block of the 'Old Polish battle-array' (see diagram on p.43). It could number from 150 to 1,500 horses, depending on its place in the battle order.

By western standards these formations were quite shallow – Hetman Florian Zebrzydowski, in his *Military Articles* of 1561, thought that even for the larger *hufs* 'there is no need to form more than four ranks [deep]'. However, since he wished to have only *towarzysze* in the front rank, each of whom at this date had five or more *pacholiks*, formations were somewhat deeper in practice. During the 1580 Russian campaign some formations were drawn up four deep, others five, while the king ordered the hussars of the Court Army under their hetman, Zborowski, to be drawn up only three deep; Zborowski himself commented that this was because they were 'older' (i.e. more experienced) troops (*WZ* 5, p. 97).

The larger *hufy* were cumbersome bodies, and in *c.*1545 Stanislaw Laski (a veteran of French and Hungarian service, who had fought at

ABOVE **By 1600 firearms were rapidly replacing bows in Poland, and the wheellock pistol and carbine had become so widespread that recorded gun crimes outnumbered those from swords. This anonymous mid-17th-century engraving depicts a typical East European horsemen, perhaps a *pacholik* (retainer) of hussars, who would be virtually indistinguishable from lighter cavalrymen when off duty or not wearing armour. His long overgarment and the top of his fur-lined cap would be of plain woollen cloth, usually made from material provided by his *towarzysz*.**

Pavia in 1525), suggested that for flexibility some should be deployed in their constituent companies. *Siekane hufy*, 'chopped *hufs*', are mentioned soon after. Hetman Jan Tarnowski in early drafts of his famous military manual *Consilium rationis bellicae* (1558) also advocated the use of smaller *hufy* of 100, 200 or 300 horses, which could be combined into larger ones when necessary, and Kircholm (1605) was won with *hufy* of 150–400 horses.

In the 1620s and 1630s, confrontation with Swedish firepower demonstrated the need to reform the Polish battle order. Western multi-line formations were copied, with hussars interspersed among infantry, artillery and other cavalry units along each line. At Beresteczko (1651) the Polish army was drawn up by veterans of the Thirty Years War (1618–48) and had an infantry centre and cavalry – including the hussars – on the wings, deployed in 'squadrons' each of six companies.

The shortage of hussars in the late 1650s led to them being parcelled out to appear more numerous. Each hussar company was broken up into three parts, and a company of *pancerni-kozaks* was deployed behind each part. By Vienna, with more hussars again available, companies ceased to be split, and each was fielded with two *pancerny* units in support, one on each flank.

Thinner formations were adopted as the average hussar *poczet* declined in size: three deep was the norm by the 1620s. Dupont suggests two deep already at Vienna, but Dalérac and other sources indicate many units were still forming three deep. After 1700 (when Dupont was writing) formations were indeed two deep, and better-armed retainers were brought into the front rank to fight alongside the *towarzysze*. This must have annoyed the proud *towarzysze* greatly – Karwicki notes in 1710 that they regarded it a 'dishonour' even to stand in the same formation with their retainers.

In battle, the best of the camp servants were formed up a few hundred paces to the rear of the main battle order, with a small flag (*znaczek*) for each formation. Shrewd commanders – such as Chodkiewicz at Kircholm – used them to imitate reinforcements, but their main duty was to feed forward spare lances (when available) and fresh horses to the parent formation, and to care for the wounded. In difficult battles such as Basia/Basheya River (1660), they did sometimes fight.

THE EXPERIENCE OF BATTLE

The hours before battle were a time for solemn reflection, which began in camp with Holy Mass. Although most Poles were Christians, pagan pre-battle superstitions remained popular: Pasek mentions soldiers 'seasoning their swords and bullets by rubbing with various holy things'. During fast-moving operations when there was no time for Mass, as at Polonka against the Russians in 1660, Pasek comments: 'While marching everyone conducted his own private service – singing, reciting prayers; our chaplains on horseback riding to hear confessions; everyone prepared himself to be as ready as possible for death.' Once in their battle formations soldiers were strictly forbidden from leaving them. The advance to combat usually began after the army had sung the traditional battle hymn (known since the 13th century): *Bogurodzica* (Mother of God).

The early phase of a battle was one of manoeuvre for advantage. The 'Old Polish battle-array' was designed for this, the hetman feeling around

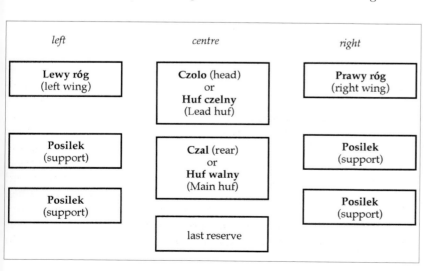

left	*centre*	*right*
Lewy róg (left wing)	**Czolo** (head) or **Huf czelny** (Lead huf)	**Prawy róg** (right wing)
Posilek (support)	**Czal** (rear) or **Huf walny** (Main huf)	**Posilek** (support)
Posilek (support)		**Posilek** (support)
	last reserve	

LEFT **The 'Old Polish battle-array' was the standard deployment used until the 1620s. All illustrations of it are idealized: actual arrangements depended on troops available and terrain. The two central blocks – each up to 1,500 strong – contained the best-equipped horsemen, with the *Huf walny* (German: *Gewalthaufen*) intended for delivering the decisive blow. The wing and support *hufs* were usually 150–300 strong. A 'last reserve' – variously named in the sources – was kept unengaged to extract the army if the action went badly.**

RIGHT **King Jan Kazimierz (1609–72) leads a hussar charge against the Ukrainian Cossack rebels and their Tatar allies at Beresteczko (1651). Many details are stylized in this 19th-century engraving of the king's funerary monument at Saint-Germain-des-Prés Church, Paris. The wings, as is often the case, have morphed into a 'natural' shape, but the fur caps worn instead of helmets by the rear ranks reflect genuine equipment shortages in the 1650s and 1660s.**

the enemy flanks with the flank *hufs*, or concentrating the 'support' *hufs* on one wing to reinforce an attack. Such concentrations were often achieved behind the cover of a skirmish screen.

Manoeuvre was performed in open order. Various 'hetman's articles' – standing orders issued by a commander – indicate that spacings between horses should be loose enough to allow units to turn 90 and 180 degrees on the spot, and Sarnicki mentions the main cavalry *huf* turned around at Obertyn (1531) using the Laconian (Spartan) counter-march. Western writers indicate that 6ft of ground per mount was enough to achieve such formation changes.

Attacks, when they came, would be rapid and aggressive, giving the enemy no time to recover balance. They were often paved by close fire-support from *haiduk* infantry (ferried around the field on nags or double-mounted behind hussars at Lubieszów, 1577) and later by dragoons on their own horses (as at Warka, 1656, where a Swedish mounted force was defeated by the dragoon-hussar combination alone). Cavalry of the *pancerny-kozak* type also helped 'shoot in' hussar charges with their long-barrelled firearms, employing a variant of the caracole of western harquebusiers, and absorbing some of the enemy fire in the process.

The charge

Lancers began their charge at about 100 paces from the enemy, and according to the famous general Montecuccoli (*Sulle battaglia*, p. 146) 'at 50 paces they run at full bridle in order to deliver their thrust'. Giorgio Basta – who had extensive experience of East European heavy hussars – wrote in his 1612 manual that lancers should 'commence their free rein at 60 paces' ... '60 paces is as much as the horse can endure so as not to arrive tired and without vigour; furthermore, the shorter the gallop, the better united will be the troop'.

A theory has developed in recent years that hussars conducted half the charge in loose formation, and closed up knee-to-knee just before the final spurt, so minimizing missile casualties and allowing the charge to be aborted at the last moment. This theory, apparently introduced by the historian J. Teodorczyk in 1966, flies in the face of all western cavalry doctrine. Western writers insist that the entire charge be conducted in tight order, as cavalry formations tend to spread out when horses gallop, with braver riders dashing ahead, and cautious or poorly mounted men falling behind.

A clear description of actual Polish practice appears in a 'Hetman's Ordinance' of *c*.1704, probably issued by Crown Grand Hetman Hieronim Lubomirski. Here it is stated that the formation manoeuvres in loose order, but *before* a charge is initiated the *rotmistrz* shouts the following series of orders:

Uciszcie sie – Silence!
Nacisniejcie czapki – Secure your hats! [this applied to 'men without metal helmets, for it is odious and inconvenient to lose one's hat in action']
Scisniejcie kolano z kolanem – Close up knee-to-knee!
Szable na temblaki – Sabres on sword-knots!
[… or for those without lances]
Szable w reku – Draw sabres!

On the order *Dalej* – March on! – the formation was to advance at a gentle trot until about half way to the enemy, at which point came the final instruction:

Zlozcie kopie – Lower your lances!

The lance was lowered alongside the horse's head, and the unit charged, now at full gallop, to contact the enemy. These instructions indicate unambiguously that the tightening of formation occurred not during the charge, but before it began. The idea that hussars could alter formation even during a charge is clearly a myth.

Interestingly, the same hetman's ordinance indicates that sabres dangled during the charge from a sword-knot, even when the rider was holding his lance. Hussars also kept their lances rested in a supporting boot or sleeve, known by the Hungarian term *tok*. Western lancers removed their lances from this before the charge, resting the lance-butt on the saddle until it was lowered shortly before contact. Polish hussars appear to have kept theirs in the *tok* even at impact. This is clear in Rakowski's *Pobudka zacnym synom (Reveille to worthy sons)* of 1620, where there are also additional instructions for the charging hussar:

The *tok* should by strapped to the saddle, on the right side; while the lance in true hussar style, should be in its *tok*. Don't twist to your left, but sit bolt upright … Over the horse's neck lower your lance; charge forward, stroking the flying beast beneath you with the spur, and aim at the enemy's navel.

Before closing with most opponents the hussars would have to endure at least one volley of enemy fire. Its effects are described at Kokenhusen (1601) by the Swedish commander Carl Gyllenhjelm, who was on the receiving end of a hussar charge. He relates how the fire from the arquebuses and carbines of the Swedish cavalry seemed to have great effect:

> Both man and horse with their lances and kopia tumbling head-over-heels to the ground. Nevertheless, those who remained uninjured and still mounted, continued on through the dust … and put our left wing to flight.

The moment of impact of lancers must have been terrifying for those on the receiving end. The sight of a few colleagues impaled on lances was often enough to shatter enemy morale. The historian Wespazjan Kochowski, in his *Song of Vienna liberated* (1684), describes the charge at Vienna (which he witnessed) in the following terms:

> No sooner does a hussar lower his lance
> Than a Turk is impaled on its spike,
> Which not only disorders, but terrifies the foe.
> That blow which cannot be defended against or deflected …
> Oft transfixing two persons at a time,
> Others flee in eager haste from such a sight,
> Like flies in a frenzy.

Modern Polish historians have accepted such quotes at face value, even though they are usually poetic; westerners have long been more sceptical about the lance's efficacy in battle. François de La Noue (p. 201), who commanded a lancer company in France during the 1570s, considered the lance charge as more bravado than effect: 'for at the onset [impact] it killeth none. Yea, it is a miracle if any be slayne with the speare [i.e. lance]: onely it may wound some horse.'

Against an enemy in plate armour the lance was not deadly, even in Poland. After the battle of Dirschau in August 1627, the Danzig secretary Johann Chemnitz reported 'the [hussar] lances were able to do little against the [Swedish] breastplates, whereas so many of them broke that they [the Poles] were encumbered by wood when they needed to come away again' (State Archive Gdansk, 300, IX, Nr.67). The Swedish colonel Clas Dietrich received his noble name 'Sperreuter' (Lancer) after an action in 1627 in which no fewer than three hussar lances broke against his armour.

Being hollowed to reduce weight, the *kopia* was even less effective than the

BELOW **'Wingless' Polish hussar, providing a unique view of the** *tok* **or leather shoe in which the lance rested even when lowered during the charge. The** *tok* **is of rounded conical shape and is attached by a broad strap to the saddle pommel. Note also the flat Tatar-style stirrups and the (faint) cross device on the two-tailed pennant. Detail of the frontispiece of** *Florus Polonicus* **(Leiden 1641) by the Silesian historian Joachim Pastorius.**

heavy western lance and was expected to break on impact; the Polish term is *kruszyc*, 'shatter or crumble', which alone indicates the weapon's fragility. Western authorities on tournaments even ridiculed the 'empty vaunting with hollow staves', which were of little danger to opponents.

The lance was a more efficient killer against less well-armoured Turkish and Russian horsemen and against their horses, and western writers stress the target of the lance in combat should be the enemy horse. Polish sources often state the rider as the target; whether this was from love of horses or from a reluctance to kill valuable loot is unclear.

The hussar lance is perhaps best understood as a psychological weapon. It was not expected to kill or maim large numbers of the enemy, but rather to destroy their morale. Conditioned as we are by Hollywood depictions of battle as mass duels, it is easy to forget that the primary aim of combat in this period was to break up enemy formations, converting a mutually supporting block of soldiers into a flock of frightened individuals who can easily be slaughtered. Montecuccoli, who commanded an Austrian corps in Poland in 1658 (*Sulle Battaglie*, p. 147), states this clearly: 'Horsed troops cannot be routed unless they are smashed open in a vigorous manner.' Montecuccoli believed that lancers were the best possible weapon for this task, though he thought they needed to be armoured from head to toe, and on good horses, and the attack needed to be followed up by cuirassiers to complete the job.

Polish hussars fit the bill perfectly, and the 'follow-through' was performed by further bodies of hussars, who were as well armoured as most Thirty Years War cuirassiers. In later years, as hussars grew scarcer, the 'follow-through' was delegated to *pancerni-kozak* horse, who may not have packed the same punch as cuirassiers, but were quicker at chasing down a beaten opponent.

Close combat

Let us assume, however, that the first hussar charge has failed to 'smash open' the enemy. Hussars who had broken their lances would reach for a secondary weapon. Indeed, with the enemy upon them, front rankers with

ABOVE **Hussars defeat carbine- and pistol-armed Swedish cavalry at Kokenhusen in Latvia (1601). It was far from certain that lancers would always beat pistolier cavalry – morale factors were always important, and formations usually disintegrated from the rear (as here). The Poles are deployed in a *huf* formation, with the constituent companies (each marked by a standard) drawn up side by side. All hussars, including those in rear ranks, carry lances. From a 19th-century copy of a print made by J. Lauro in 1603 for Hetman-chancellor Jan Zamoyski; the only known original was destroyed in Warsaw in 1944.**

ABOVE **Hussar *towarzysz* of c.1600–20 from the Goluchów 'costume tableau'. His armour has still not evolved into a recognizably 'Polish' form: the helmet has gilded cheek-pieces, while the breastplate is an early 'half-lobster' variety with four lames (gilded on the upper surfaces), worn with mail sleeves but no mail skirt or armguards. The animal pelt appears to have been dyed with spots to make it appear like a leopard. The short summer zupan coat (the commonest form of male overgarment) is of bright red cloth, as are the tight hussar trousers, which button up the side. Note also the *nadziak* war-hammer with its square head.**

unbroken lances would have little option but to drop their lances as well. It was not the *koncerz* nor the *pallash* to which they turned first: in the few frantic seconds that constituted cavalry combat in this period, it took too long to draw from its scabbard on the saddle.

Some might reach for pistols, though De La Noue (p. 201) considered the single pistol carried by lancers in his day as ineffective – often misfiring since the rider was too preoccupied with his lance to attend to the temperamental mechanism. Others might grasp a war-hammer: these were excellent for piercing helmets and armour, although Malatesta (1610), a particular fan of Polish war-hammers, thought they were best reserved for duels rather than combat, since they were 'not very handy in striking, nor easy to retrieve' (after delivering a blow). The bulk of hussars, however, took to their sabres, which hung on a sword knot from the wrist during the charge. (The *koncerz* was too cumbersome to be held in this manner.)

Against pistol-armed cavalry the hussars would now find themselves at a disadvantage; as De La Noue notes 'the Reistres are never so daungerous as when they bee mingled with the enemie, for then be they all fire.' It was preferable to withdraw for another charge while some lances were still intact. A few sabre slashes, and the 'contact' was quickly over.

Tactics were planned with multiple charges in mind. Not all companies charged at the same time; some remained stationary at the rear awaiting the outcome of the first 'wave'. A hussar company that had failed to break its opponents returned to its lines through intervals left by supporting units. These intervals, notes the 1704 Hetman's Ordinance, were to be at least as wide as the formation itself.

Sheltering behind its supports, our hussar company now caught breath, reordered ranks and prepared for the next charge. Any unbroken lances were passed forward to the front rank. Sobieski, in a letter to his wife, relates how at the second battle of Parkany in October 1683 he ordered those hussars still with lances to move forward to the front rank. A commotion ensued, in which a *pacholik* rode in front of his master and complained loudly: 'Your honour, I brought the lance out of battle for myself; I didn't throw it down like others.' Greatly amused, Sobieski gave the wily trooper five gold ducats.

Those without lances now unsheathed their *koncerz* or *pallash* from beneath the saddle; indeed Pasek (in his description of the Basheya River Battle, 1660) indicates that this was the regulation: 'Anyone who had broken his lance was to take to their *pallash*, such was the standing order.' The *koncerz* could be used as a pseudo-lance, its great length and evil point unnerving the enemy, threatening to skewer even those skulking on the ground out of sabre-reach, but it was less useful in a mêlée. As anyone who has held a *koncerz* will testify, the weapon is blade-heavy, making parrying with it awkward. The *pallash* – the equivalent of the western cavalry broadsword – was far more popular. Being designed for the thrust, it could be employed in tighter formations than the sabre. In battle descriptions where hussars have already broken their lances, it is usually with a *pallash* as their main weapon: 'Soon after breaking our *kopia* on them, again we attacked Moscow with our *pallashes*.' (The soldier-poet Andrzej Rymsza describing an action in 1580.)

So the battle continued, with a wave-like effect, companies charging, retiring, re-forming and then charging again, until one side finally gave way. At Klushino (1610) Maskiewicz, a *towarzysz* with one of the most heavily engaged hussar units, wrote: 'it may be hard to believe, but some companies came to contact and fought with the enemy eight or ten times.' This was clearly atypical. Nevertheless, at Górzno (1629) a short, unsuccessful engagement, Swedish witnesses record that some hussar companies managed to charge three or four times.

Hussars versus pikemen

Hussars, like all good-quality cavalry, could easily overrun infantry formations in the open if they were unprotected by pikes. However, the idea has grown over the last few decades that even pikes were insufficient to protect infantry from the long lances of the hussars. This has been set firmly in the popular imagination by Hoffman's film *The Deluge*, where hussars (un-historically) ride down Swedish pikemen in 1656.

First, there is the idea that hussar lances were lengthened specifically to outreach pikes. This is far from proven. Until the end of the Swedish War in 1629, Polish lances (about 5m long) appear to have been shorter than Swedish pikes, which had a regulation length of 5.98m, reduced in 1616 to 5.3m. Indeed, it is only later in the century that writers like Cefali (1660s), Fredro (1670) and Dalérac (1690s) commented that the *kopia* was 'longer than our infantry pikes'. But this was because the pikes had shrunk by this date to a more manageable 14–16ft (4.2–4.8m). Even if this were not the case, what advantage was an extra foot or two of lance when a split second later the horse's momentum impaled it on the dense hedge of pikes?

In fact the few successes of hussars against pikemen occurred before 1629. There are far fewer of them than the legend suggests, and the hussars rarely achieved victory unassisted. For example, at Lubieszów (1577) during the Danzig Rebellion, 3,000 German landsknechts were routed by hussars, but only after they had been engaged frontally by 600 Hungarian *haiduk* infantry of the royal guard. Nor were other famous victories such as Pitschen (1588) and Klushino (1610) achieved by the direct charges of hussars on steady pikemen.

The single exception is Kircholm (1605), where about 3,500 Lithuanians managed to trounce a Swedish army of nearly 11,000. But these were not the immaculately trained troops of Gustavus Adolphus. The native Swedish infantry were virtually unarmoured, still reluctant to 'trail' the pike and poorly trained in its use.[1] However, that the hussars did indeed charge pikemen at Kircholm is recorded, for example, in the broadsheet *Nowiny z Inflant* (*News from Livonia*), written soon after the battle: 'They [the hussars] fell on the pikemen, since it could not be otherwise, and broke through the enemy, though not without damage to themselves.' Kircholm was an astounding tribute to Polish arms. Even the Poles recognized its uniqueness. Jakub Sobieski, father of the future king, later wrote: 'In future centuries the victory will be marvelled at, rather than actually believed.' But it would be quite wrong to generalize from a single battle that the Polish lance was a super-weapon never seen anywhere else in the history of warfare, which allowed hussars to break pikemen as a matter of routine.

See R. Brzezinski, *The Army of Gustavus Adolphus (1): Infantry*, Osprey MAA 235, p. 18.

Pursuit

Wars in Eastern Europe have long been brutal affairs; those in 17th-century Poland were little different. Polish armies were usually outnumbered, and commanders understood the need to reduce enemy manpower at every opportunity. Hetman Florian Zebrzydowski's *Military Articles* of 1561 state that during battle cavalry were not to take prisoners unless they looked important. The leading pursuers were to inflict disabling wounds on the enemy and not to trouble with killing them, but to ride on looking for more enemy. The wounded would be dispatched by camp servants following behind.

After Lubieszów (1577) half the 8,000 Danzig citizen militia who had done little more than stand by as spectators during the action were butchered during their rout – arousing bitterness in the Polish Commonwealth's largest city for decades to come. After Kircholm at least half and perhaps as much as two-thirds of the Swedish army were killed during the retreat – more than two Swedes for every Pole at the battle.

The loot-hungry *pacholiks* and camp servants were especially feared by the enemy. At Basheya River (1660) Pasek was mistaken for a retainer by a Russian boyar who was attempting to surrender:

> I looked untrustworthy, being dressed in a grey *kontusz*; he distrusts me, thinking me a *pacholik*, worthless rabble, the sort which are most feared: they say you never find generosity in such people (as he himself later related). But in the distance he saw a

RIGHT **The battle of Kircholm in 1605 was one of the only occasions when Polish hussars destroyed western pike-and-shot formations unaided. When charged, the musketeers fell back under the shelter of the pikes, creating a 'soft cushion' in front of the pikes, which the hussars could attempt to disorder without impaling themselves on the pikes. Detail from Snayers' painting of the battle.**

towarzysz, one of ours, but dressed in red in a tatty old crimson *kontusz* ... he supposed this was a person of note and rode straight to him [to offer his surrender].

Even so, if Russian nobles survived capture they could be exceptionally well treated. Polish diaries are full of accounts of merry drink-filled evenings shared with Russian prisoners, and of friendships springing up that both parties promised to maintain when the conflict was over.

Casualties

After the battle of Klushino, Maskiewicz records the fate of the Polish dead and wounded as follows: 'The hetman ordered all our casualties collected into a heap and the more prominent ones, like the *towarzysze*, he had taken with him, the rest were buried. The wounded and shot *towarzysze* he had placed in his own carriage or carried on a stretcher between two horses.'

Hussar *towarzysze*, seldom having surgeons on their company strength, generally received the care of the hetman's personal physician, often a foreigner or a Pole who had studied medicine abroad. Their retainers had to make do with whatever traditional remedies the camp servants could concoct. Badly wounded hussars also received far higher compensation than other troops – in 1649 after the epic siege of Zbaraz, they were given 250 *zloty*, compared to 90 for *pancerny-kozaks* and only 30 for infantrymen.

Casualty statistics survive for many Polish victories. Dead and wounded *towarzysze* are often mentioned by name along with the numbers of horses each company lost and even types of wounds the men suffered. It was rare for a 100-horse hussar company to lose more than four *towarzysze* and eight retainers killed or wounded. Horse losses were approximately double those of the men. Generally speaking, casualties from firearms greatly outnumbered those from cold-steel weapons.

However, it is dangerous to generalize from these figures that hussars were relatively invulnerable. Acts of unit heroism often resulted in more extreme casualties. During the victory over the Russians at Szklów in 1654 Janusz Radziwill's hussar company is reported to have lost more than half of its strength in an exhausting five-hour action. At Vienna in 1683, Prince Alexander Sobieski's company lost 19 *towarzysze* and 36 retainers of its 120–130 actual men during its charge to test the ground prior to the main assault (see Plate G). The often crippling casualties from Polish defeats are less well recorded.

ABOVE **Polish cavalry boot, one of a pair, made c.1665 for Carl XI of Sweden as a boy (Livrustkammaren 06/5900). They are of yellow morocco leather (saffian) with flesh side out, have turnshoe soles and broad white stitching in the vamp seam and heel seat, and are straights (identical right and left), 20cm long × 40cm maximum height. The metal heels consist of a horseshoe-shaped iron tube, 3–4mm thick and 25mm high. Such heels were a source of amusement to westerners: 'When they [Poles] take a walk in the garden it seems by the marks they leave with their heels in the paths that a flock of sheep have passed' (Relation d'un voiage de Pologne fait ... 1688 et 1689, Paris 1858, p. 80).**

AFTER BATTLE

Most campaigns drew to a close in late autumn, as the first snows began to fall. With their wagons empty, horses lacking fodder and ill-nourished troops suffering illness, few armies would remain useful in the field over winter. If no action was expected the following spring and funds were available to pay troops off, companies were generally disbanded. This was not the end of them. The next campaign was seldom a year or more away, and a *rotmistrz* would receive a fresh recruitment letter from the king and revive his unit from a dormant state – largely with the same men – to serve in another campaign.

After the army reforms of 1652, companies began to have a more permanent existence, aided by the almost permanent state of war that had engulfed Poland. In the rare years of peace companies were reduced to 60–80 horses rather than being disbanded, while the hetmans maintained units of 100 or more. Many companies endured for decades, developing strong corporate identities. Companies shared the fortunes of their patron. Aleksander Skorobohaty (1639–99) served for ten years in various *pancerni* units before joining the hussar company of Lithuanian Grand Hetman Pawel Sapieha in 1665, only to see it disbanded after the hetman's death in the following year. He signed on three days later in the company of Lithuanian Field Hetman Mikolaj Kazimierz Pac, who in 1667 was promoted to Grand Hetman. After Pac died in 1682 the company was taken over by Jan Sobieski, becoming his royal hussar company of the Lithuanian army. Skorobohaty now found himself in the highest-status company in the land.

Demotions in unit status also occurred when a *rotmistrz* died. If a wealthy patron could not be found to take over the company quickly, the company often broke up. There was nothing to prevent a *towarzysz* from enlisting with a different *rotmistrz*; such transfers were possible after the completion of every quarter year of service. Ambitious individuals switched regularly between units, starting in *pancerni-kozak* cavalry and gradually working their way up to a high-status unit of hussars, the pinnacle of ambition being to serve in the king's own hussar company – under the eyes, and hopefully favours, of the monarch.

Retirement

For many hussars their military service was merely a rite of passage, a short interlude in their life as noblemen. It won them the respect of peers and the clubbish camaraderie of a noble class who still referred to themselves as 'knights'. A professional career might last considerably longer, and several diarists write of their retirement after 20 years of field service. Skorobohaty served no fewer than 37 years, retiring at the age of 52 in 1691, though after 1684 he no longer went on campaign, having left his *poczet* in the charge of his retainers.

The Seym committed itself in 1607 to reward soldiers who had served six years (*VL* 2, f.1629). In practice hussar *towarzysze* were often granted the semi-hereditary post of *wójt* or headman of a village or small town, which gave considerable status and power. This post was ideally suited to the incidental skills learned on campaign – haggling with civil and military officials

BELOW **Hussars with saddle-mounted wings, leopard skins and *welens* capes at the armed 'demonstration' prior to the signing of the Peace of Altmark with Sweden in 1635. Such events were opportunities for the hussars to dress in all their finery and wings with the aim of overawing the Swedish commissioners. Ceiling panel by Tomasso Dollabella, painted *c.*1640 for the palace of one of the Polish peace delegates, Bishop Jakub Zadzik. (Bishop's Palace, Kielce)**

over quarters and pay arrears. Many retired hussars went on to careers in national government. In times of major crisis, when the *Pospolite Ruszenie* (noble levy) was called out, former hussars were brought out of retirement to command levy units.

As Poland's financial situation deteriorated in the later 17th century, service rewards were cut back or granted mostly to members of royal units. The hussar Poczobut-Odlanicki was disbanded in October 1671 after over 12 years of service. Having taken part in many parades himself he was distressed that his 'de-mobbing' took place without any ceremony. He had been promised the post of *wójt*, but the civil offices went only to the officers of his unit. Although many retired hussars bemoaned the lack of financial rewards, most merely lamented the many horses they had lost on campaign, and wrote about them at length in their memoirs composed in their autumn years.

The hussars had evolved a unique funerary ritual as a fitting farewell to former companions and commanders. At the culmination of the funeral service a fully armoured hussar representing the deceased rode full tilt into the church and splintered his lance against the altar. By the 18th century hussars rarely set forth on campaign and the only time the public ever saw these 'funereal soldiers', as Kitowicz called them, was in such ceremonies.

ABOVE **Two hussars from the sketchbook of the Italian painter Martino Altomonte, who was commissioned in the 1690s to produce battle paintings for King John Sobieski. Though the hussars are without wings, they have plumed *szyszak* helmets and leopardskins. (Benediktinerstift Melk, Austria)**

DEMISE OF THE HUSSARS

By 1600 the heavy lancer was obsolete in western Europe. Only a few companies remained in service as generals' honour guards into the 1630s. With its flat plains and vast distances Poland was more suited to lancers than many countries, but the end of the golden age of the hussar was not long in coming.

Above all it was the massive firepower of the reformed troops of Gustavus Adolphus that put an end to the hussar's ascendancy. The first sign of problems came at Mitau in Latvia in August 1622 where, facing a wall of fire from Swedish field guns and musketeers, the hussars flatly refused to charge. The Lithuanian hetman Krzysztof Radziwill wrote: 'I rode from one cavalry unit to the next … said I would lead them myself, threatened them with the gallows, promised them rewards, but nothing helped.' (K. Radziwill, *Sprawy wojenne i polityczne*, p. 282). Similar scenes were repeated at Gniew/Mewe (1626) in Polish Prussia.

Even the pistol-armed Swedish cavalry were no longer a pushover, and after Dirschau in 1627, Chemnitz commented that the relative ineffectiveness of the Polish lancers in the battle will 'hopefully give them cause to rearm in the Netherlandish manner, with arquebuses and good pistols.' During the 'Deluge' of 1655–58 the hussars avoided frontal assaults on the Swedes, with their tightly intersecting fields of fire from muskets and quick-firing artillery. The partly successful hussar charge at Warsaw (1656) was directed against a

Swedish cavalry wing, but that too was repulsed with the help of infantry and artillery fire.

The hussars were becoming an anachronism when fighting westernized armies such as the Swedes, but until the end of the 17th century they continued to be of value against eastern opponents such as the Russians and the Turks. However, their direct cost to the state was far higher than their paltry salary, which increasingly was not being paid. On a costly steed that took three months or more to train, employing an expensive lance that could be used only once, and with a vast staff of servants who clogged up roads and camps, consuming the limited supplies of food and fodder, they were hardly an effective use of scarce resources.

The gradual demoralization of Polish society from the 1650s, which spilled over into the army, was just as much of a problem. A 100-horse company of hussars represented 30–40 *towarzysze* – each in effect an officer with his own opinion, which he voiced at every opportunity. Any system in which these argumentative gentlemen dined with their commanders as equals was hardly conducive to military discipline. They could ignore orders from officers of western-style formations (whom they regarded as riff-raff), and had to be convinced by their own commanders to charge rather than be ordered to do so.

In their heyday the *husaria* had won some of history's most decisive victories. Their visual splendour, whether their wings were saddle-

BELOW **The famous charge on the second day of the battle of Warsaw, 29–31 July 1656, in which 1,000–1,500 Polish and Lithuanian hussars smashed through the first line of the Swedish left (cavalry) wing, but, inadequately supported, were repulsed by the reserve lines and supporting infantry and artillery. Detail of a print engraved in 1686, from eyewitness sketches by the Swedish engineer Erik Dahlberg.**

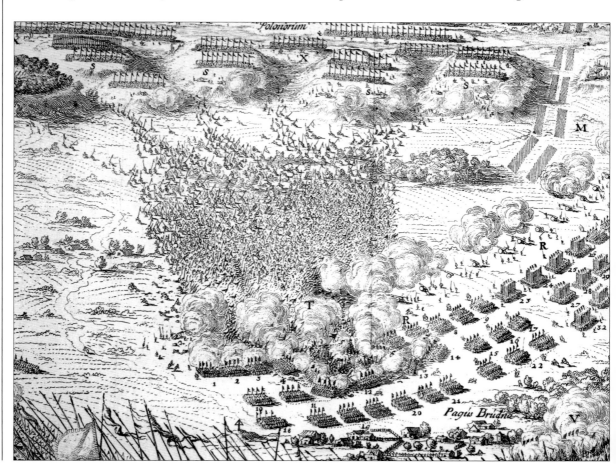

mounted or back-mounted, made a dazzling impression on all who saw them. The Polish hussars were certainly among the finest cavalry of their day, but the words of Sobieski's one-time doctor, Bernard Connor (Ch. VI, p. 9), are perhaps a more accurate epitaph: 'These [hussars], were they but better Disciplin'd and better paid, would perhaps be the finest Cavalry in the World.'

Finally, in 1775, the Seym abolished the hussars. Those men still fit for service were reorganized into new brigades of unarmoured 'National Cavalry' (*Kawaleria Narodowa*). The future now belonged to more plebeian formations that were cheaper to equip and better able to replace casualties. Chief among these were the Uhlans, which had evolved out of Tatar cavalry in Polish service. In this more mobile guise – and equipped with a lighter lance – the Polish lancer was again to make his mark across the battlefields of Europe.

COLLECTING

Hussar weaponry and armour rarely appears on the open market; most that does is either fake or not Polish. Genuine pieces invariably reach the attention of Polish dealers and can fetch extraordinary sums. Far more plentiful and affordable are arms and armour in Polish or Hungarian style, most of which were made in western Europe.

Buyers should be wary of modern modifications – such as Polish 'wings' welded on to otherwise mundane German Pappenheimer

LEFT **Helmets with attached metal winglets are a puzzle. They first appear in art of the 1730s when Poland was ruled by a Saxon king, and are worn only by Saxon cavalrymen – as a 'practical' alternative to the Polish back-mounted wing. Poles favoured elaborate burnished steel helmets, yet most surviving winged helmets are obsolete burgonets or (as here) mass-produced 'Pappenheimers' to which the winglets have been added. It may be a patriotic thought-crime to point this out, but there is actually little evidence that winged helmets are Polish rather than Saxon. (Polish Institute and Sikorski Museum, London)**

helmets. Any wings attached to armour suits are almost certain to be modern replicas. *Karacena* scale armour and *buzdygan* maces make occasional appearances at auctions, but for most collectors ambitions should be limited to western-made helmets, war-hammers (which were widely used throughout central and eastern Europe), and 18th-century Polish or Hungarian sabres.

ENTERTAINMENT AND RE-ENACTMENT

For those wishing to sample the flavour of the period, an excellent starting point is the trilogy of novels on Poland's 17th-century wars by Nobel laureate Henryk Sienkiewicz (1846–1916). These have been translated into English and were also made into films: *Colonel Wolodyjowski/Fire on the Steppe* (1968), *The Deluge* (1974), and *With Fire & Sword* (1998).

At the time of writing, re-enactment is still in its early days – hampered by the high cost of hussar equipment. In the USA the most active groups operate under the umbrella of the Sienkiewicz Society, in particular Boleslav Orlicki's light artillery and its affiliated bodies Czarniecki's division in CT/NY and Butler's dragoons in TX/AR (traceable with any internet search engine). A useful clearing house for information is Zagloba's Tavern: http://groups.yahoo.com/group/zaglobastavern

In Poland re-enactment is concentrated on the medieval period, with the stress on fun rather than historical accuracy. Seventeenth-century groups keen on authenticity include the Liga Baronów (League of Barons): www.ligabaronow.prv.pl and Wisniowiecki's company of *pancerni*: http://choragiewpancerna.prv.pl. A Polish board for re-enactors can be found at www.freha.pl

GLOSSARY

Choragiew	1. company flag; 2. 'company' of troops serving under the flag – the basic organizational unit of Polish cavalry.
Chorazy	standard-bearer, ensign, a junior officer rank.
Ciura	(pl. *ciury*) camp servant, see also *czeladz obozowa*.
Cossacks	1. Polish term for the emerging Ukrainian nation; 2. a class of cavalry recruited throughout Poland – see *Kozak*.
Crown	the Kingdom of Poland, heartland of the Polish–Lithuanian Commonwealth.
Czeladnik	(pl. **czeladz**) – servant of a *towarzysz*, confusingly often used of the *pacholiks/pocztowi*.
Czeladz obozowa	camp servants, also called 'loose' servants. (*czeladz luzna*) or *ciury*.
Elear	elite hussar (later *kozak*) selected from the bravest horsemen to ride ahead of the army and 'open' the battle. Comparable to the Ottoman *deli* 'madcap'.
Haiduk	infantry arquebusier equipped in Hungarian style.
Hetman	Commander (ultimately from German *Hauptman* 'captain'). Polish and Lithuanian armies were each led by a *Hetman Wielki* (Grand Hetman) and a slightly junior *Hetman Polny* (Field Hetman).
Huf	(Medieval German *Hufe*, modern German *Haufen*) the standard tactical formation of Polish cavalry until *c*.1620.
Karacena	(Italian *corazzina*) metal scale armour in antiquated 'Sarmatian' style, fashionable among hussar and *pancerni* officers from the 1670s.
Karwasze	Armguards made in oriental style.
Komput	état or establishment of the army. From 1652 state-paid forces were known as the *komputowe* army.
Koncerz	exceptionally long sword of square or triangular section, designed for piercing mail.
Kozak	(pl. **Kozacy**) light or medium cavalryman employed alongside the hussars, recruited throughout Poland–Lithuania, and known from *c*.1660 as *Pancerni*. Not to be confused

Kwarciani	with the 'Cossack nation' in the Ukraine. ('Quarter troops') soldiers of the standing army or *Wojsko kwarciane*, paid from a fraction of the royal revenues.
Pacholik	(modern Polish *pacholek*, 'youth') retainer employed by a *towarzysz*. From late 17th century known as *pocztowy*.
Pallash	(Polish **palasz**) broadsword with a sabre-type hilt, the hussar's main secondary weapon.
Pancerny	(pl. **pancerni**) medium cavalryman, named after his mail armour (*pancerz*). The term began to replace *kozak* during the Ukrainian Cossack Rebellion of 1648–54, and became general from the 1660s.
Poczet	equivalent of western 'lance'; comprising (from 1600) a *towarzysz* and 1–3 *pacholiks*, plus camp servants.
Pocztowy	(pl. **pocztowi**) – 'member of a *poczet*'; used from the late 17th century in place of *pacholik*.
Porucznik	deputy commander ('lieutenant') of a company.
Pulk	formation of several companies combined for the duration of a campaign; from the 17th century also used to translate western 'regiment'.
Pulkownik	commander of a *pulk*; usually translated as 'colonel'.
Retainer	see *pacholik*.
Rota	synonym for company (*choragiew*).
Rotmistrz	'rota-master', commander of a *rota*.
Seym	(Polish *Sejm*) the Polish diet or parliament.
Szyszak	cavalry helmet of oriental, open-faced style.
Tabor	wagon-fort, field fortification of chained wagons.
Tok	leather sleeve or shoe in which the butt of the lance rested, suspended on a strap from the saddle pommel.
Towarzysz	A gentleman-soldier, literally 'companion' (of the *rotmistrz*), supplying a *poczet*; also often translated as 'comrade'.
Welens	(pl. **Welense**) cape, often garishly striped, worn over hussar armour c.1600–50.

SELECT BIBLIOGRAPHY

Only the 'iceberg's tip' of the literature consulted is quoted here. Most works are available only in Polish; those with summaries or photo captions in a western language are marked by an asterisk (*).

Abbreviations

SMHW = *Studia i Materialy do Historii Wojskowosci*, Warsaw 1955– (periodical)

VL = *Volumina Legum*, I–IX, Petersburg 1859–60 (Acts of the Seym)

WZ = *Wypisy zrodlowe do historii polskiej sztuki wojennej*, vols. 5, 6, 7, 8A, Warsaw 1954–66 (extracts from the works of Cefali, Kampenhausen, Fredro, J. Zborowski, etc.)

Selected primary sources

Brulig, Bernard, 'Pater B. B.'s Bericht über die Belagerung der Stadt Wien im Jahre 1683', *Archiv für Kunde österreichischer Geschichtsquellen*, t.IV, 1850, pp. 424–38

Connor, Bernard, *The history of Poland in several letters to persons of quality*, London 1698

Dalérac, F. P., *Les anecdotes de Pologne*, Paris 1699

Dupont, Philippe, *Mémoires pour servir à l'histoire de la vie et des actions de Jean Sobieski III* ... Warsaw 1885

Dyakowski, M., *Dyaryusz widenskiej okazyji*, Warsaw 1983

Gyllenhjelm, C. C., 'Egenhändiga anteckningar ... 1597–1601', *Historiska Handlingar*, 20, Stockholm 1905, pp. 258–395

Karwicki, S. Dunin, *Dziela polityczne...[1703–10]*, ed. A. & K. Przybos, Wroclaw 1992

Kitowicz, J., *Opis obyczajów za panowania Augusta III*, Warsaw 1985

de La Noue, F., *The politicke and militarie discourses ...* London 1587

Los, Jakub, *Pamietnik towarzysza choragwi pancernej*, ed. R. Sreniawa-Szypiowski, Warsaw: DiG, 2000

Maskiewicz, Samuel & Boguslaw, *Pamietniki...*, ed. A. Sajkowski, Wroclaw 1961

Massario Malatesta, A., *Compendio dell'heroica arte di cavalleria*, Danzig 1610

Montecuccoli, R., 'Sulle battaglie [1639–42]', in T. M. Barker, *The Military Intellectual and Battle: Raimondo Montecuccoli and the Thirty Years War*, Albany, NY, 1975

Naronowicz-Naronski, J., *Budownictwo wojenne [1659]*, Warsaw 1957

Ogier, Charles, *Dziennik podrózy do Polski*, t.I, Gdansk 1950 – parallel Latin text

*Pawinski, A., (ed.), *Batory pod Gdanskiem (Batory at Danzig, 1576–77)*, Warsaw 1877 – documents, mostly Latin

Pasek, Jan Chrysostom, *Memoirs of the Polish Baroque*, transl. Catherine S. Leach, University of California Press, 1976

Poczobut-Odlanicki, J. W., *Pamietnik [1640–84]*, ed. A. Rachuba, Warsaw: DiG, 1987

Skorobohaty, A. D., *Diariusz [1639–99]*, ed. T. Wasilewski, Warsaw: DiG, 2000

Starowolski, S., *Eques Polonus*, Venice 1628

Starowolski, S., *Prawy Rycerz [1648]*, ed. K. J. Turowski, Kraków 1858

Secondary sources

Anglo, Sydney, *The Martial Arts of Renaissance Europe*, Yale University Press, 2000

*Bochenski, Z., 'Ze studiów nad polska zbroja husarska', *Rozprawy i sprawozdania Muzeum Narodowego w Krakowie*, 6 (1960), pp. 12–50

Bochenski, Z., 'Próba okreslenia genezy polskiej zbroi husarskiej', *Muzealnictwo Wojskowe*, 2 (1964), pp. 141–66

Brzezinski, R., 'The wings of the Polish hussars: their origin and purpose', *Military Illustrated*, No. 88 (1995), pp. 30–5

Cichowski, J. & A. Szulczynski, *Husaria*, Warsaw 1977; 2nd edition 2004

Frost, Robert I., *The Northern Wars 1558–1721*, Longman 2000

Gembarzewski, B., 'Husarze. Ubiór, oparzadzenie i uzbrojenie 1500–1775', *Bron i Barwa*, 1938, pp. 207–54 and 1939, pp. 51–70; reprint Warsaw: Arcadia, 1999

Górski, Konstanty, *Historya jazdy polskiej*, Kraków 1895

Grégoire, Henri & P. Orgels, 'Qu'est-ce qu'un "hussard", ou De l'utilite du grec moderne', *Annuaire de l'Institute de Phil. et D'Hist. Orientales et Slaves*, V (Bruxelles 1937), pp. 443–51

Jähns, M., *Geschichte der Kriegswissenschaften*, Munich & Leipzig 1889–91

Janas, E. & L. Wasilewski, 'Spoleczne aspekty rozwoju husarii w latach 1648–67…', *SMHW* 23 (1981) pp. 65–112

Kalmár, János, *Régi magyar fegyverek* (Old Hungarian Weapons), Budapest 1971

Laskowski, O., 'L'art militaire polonaise au XVIe et au XVII siecle', *Revue internationale d'histoire militaire*, 12 (1952), pp. 462–93

Nagielski, M., 'Choragwie husarskie Aleksander Hilarego Polubinskiego i króla Jana Kazimierza w latach 1648–66', *Acta Baltico-Slavica*, XV (Wroclaw 1983), pp. 77–138

Nickel, Helmut, 'Dorsal Devices: Polish Hussars' Wings, Japanese Sashimono and Aztec Tlahuitzli', in: *Congress Report: VIII Congress of Int. Assoc. of Arms and Mil. History* (Warsaw 1978), pp. 19–23

Ostrowski J., & W. Bochnak, 'Polish sabres: their origins and evolution', in R. Held (ed), *Art, Arms & Armour*, vol. I (1979–80), Chiasso 1979, pp. 220–37

Teodorczyk, J., 'Bitwa pod Gniewem 1626. Pierwsza porazka husarii', *SMHW* 12/2 (1966), pp. 70–172

Tezcan, H., 'Topkapi Saryi'ndak velense', *Topkapi Saryi Muzesi*, 5 (1992), pp. 223–40

Wagner, M., *Stanislaw Jablonowski*, Siedlce 1997, 2 vols

Wasilkowska, A., *Husaria. The Winged Horsemen*, Interpress, 1998

*Wimmer, J., *Wojsko Rzeczypospolitej w dobie Wojny Pólnocnej (1700–1717)*, Warsaw 1956

Wimmer, J., *Wojsko Polskie w drugiej polowie XVII wieku*, Warsaw 1965

Wisner, H., 'Wojsko litewskie I polowy XVII wieku', Pts 1–3 [in:] *SMHW*, vols. 19/1, 20, 21 (1973–78)

Wojtasik, J., 'Ordynacja hetmanska dotyczaca taktyki wojsk polskich z poczatku XVIII w', *SMHW*, 6/1 (1960), pp. 288–92

*Zygulski, Z., 'Ze studiow nad dawna sztuka siodlarska', *Rozprawy i Sprawozdania Muzeum Narodowego w Krakowie*, 5 (Kraków 1959), pp. 41–105

Zygulski, Z., 'The winged hussars of Poland', *Arms & Armor Annual* (ed. R.Held), vol. 1, Northfield, Illinois 1973, pp. 90–103

*Zygulski, Z., *Bron w dawnej Polsce*, Warsaw 1982

*Zygulski, Z., *Stara bron w polskich zbiorach*, Warsaw 1984

*Zygulski, Z., *Husaria Polska. The Polish Hussaria*, Warsaw 2000

COLOUR PLATE COMMENTARY

LEFT A rare realistic depiction of an early armoured hussar, from the tombstone of Piotr Strzela, a Moravian who died in 1600. The inscription (in Czech) states he died aged 40 'in the Polish Crown', suggesting he had served in Poland. His equipment, which unusually for Polish funerary sculpture shows little stylization, includes a fully articulated 'lobster' breastplate, mail sleeves and skirt, and a war-hammer. See plate A for a reconstruction. (St Bartholomew's Church, Sucha, near Strzelce Opolskie, Poland)

without the characteristic brass decorations. His breastplate is of 'full lobster' or 'anima' style, reconstructed from a similar example in the National Museum, Budapest. A type of breastplate with a high gorget [2] appears to have been more common; this example is taken from a large batch of such armours made in Styria in the 1590s and surviving to this day in the Graz Armoury in Austria. Note the leather lining, which is partly original. An alternative form of helmet of similar date [3] is also from Graz, with the leather lining [3a] reconstructed from another surviving helmet.

Though this hussar wears a mail shirt under his armour, the requirement was only for mail sleeves. Written sources sometimes mention 'zarekawie z ksztaltem' – mail sleeves attached to an arming garment [4], which we reconstruct from a hussar in a Roelant Savery painting of c.1605 and mail sleeves from Graz.

The various types of war-hammer [5] were known at first indiscriminately as a czekan (from Hungarian csákany). Only towards 1700 did the term nadziak (from Turkish nacak) come into use to describe the variant with a hammer-head and an extended beak carried by our central figure.

Combat sabres [6] were still of open-hilted Hungarian style, but had lost the heavy blades of Hungarian weapons. Increasingly, a chainlet was added to protect the knuckle. The scabbard was of wood lined with black leather, and hung from a waist belt on two (sometimes four) slings [7], which were adjustable with the help of slider fittings [7a]. On campaign, sabres were fitted with a sword-knot (temblak) [8], here taken from a portrait.

Tall and short varieties of Hungarian moroccan leather boots [9] were fashionable among hussars; both had horseshoe-shaped hollow metal heels. Combat spurs were now of simple Western form; long spurs [10] were reserved mostly for parades.

B: COMPANY OF COURTIERS (CHORAGIEW DWORZAÑSKA), 1605
At the heart of the royal guard was a hussar formation raised from minor state functionaries and courtiers (dworzanie), each of whom equipped a 'courtier retinue' of four to 24 hussars. The combined unit has for decades been misnamed as the 'Royal hussar company': its correct name is the 'Company of Courtiers' (Choragiew Dworzañska). This is the main hussar unit depicted on the Stockholm roll (see page 60).

In the regular army each hussar company used a single design of pennant. The Courtier Company was different, with each courtier retinue having its own pennant and lance design in an elaborate range of patterns; all 12 designs shown on the

A: HUSSAR TOWARZYSZ, 1590s
The re-arming of the Polish hussars in Hungarian style was set in motion by King Stefan Batory in 1576, but took until the 1590s to implement across the Polish–Lithuanian Commonwealth.

The central figure [1] shows such a 'Hungarian' style hussar, taken from the tombstone of Piotr Strzela (see above). His headgear has the basic form of later Polish helmets, but roll are reconstructed here for the first time. Each courtier retinue also had its own style of cape or leopardskin and helmet decoration (with varying numbers/types of plumes, presence/absence of a spike or gilding).

The hussar *towarzysz* [1] with star-spangled panther skin is taken from row 4 front of the Stockholm Roll (for the arrangement of retinues on the roll, see the illustration opposite). His *szyszak* helmet is of an early form with an adjustable visor but no nasal, and appears to be a bulk issue for the whole company.

All retinues wear mail shirts below their breastplates (or mail sleeves and separate mail skirts), but no armguards or gauntlets. Each hussar has two swords – a sabre and a *pallash* broadsword – the scabbard decorations not always matching. The extra-long *koncerz* sword is conspicuously absent. Wings are of frame variety, worn singly on the left side of the saddle only. There are no clear images of the saddle attachment; we reconstruct a possible method.

The opposite schematics show courtier retinues with *welense* capes. They are [2] from row 6 front, [3*] row 5

BELOW **The Hussar Company of Courtiers (*choragiew dworzańska*) from the 'Stockholm Roll' – so-called because it spent several centuries in Sweden after being looted in Warsaw in 1655–56. The 15m-long roll depicts the parade held in Kraków for the wedding of Zygmunt III Waza and the Habsburg princess Constance in December 1605. Accounts of the event record that the company numbered 200–300 hussars, but give only generalized descriptions of the unit's appearance. Only rows 1–5 of the seven depicted are shown here. (Royal Castle, Warsaw)**

back, [4] row 3, and [5*] row 7 back. The pennants marked with an asterisk are partly hidden on the original, and our reconstructions, although sometimes speculative, are based on all possible clues, including pennant length and shape.

C: COMPANY OF COURTIERS (CONTINUED)

The figures in this plate all represent courtier retinues wearing leopardskins. [1] is taken from row 7 front of the Stockholm Roll. He is one of the few figures in the Courtier Company wearing a 'half-lobster' breastplate with just three or four lames at the waist (reconstructed from an example in the Graz Armoury dated 1595). Most of the company wear the older 'full-lobster' breastplates (see Plate A). Both styles have tall gorgets covering much of the neck.

The spikes shown on the helmets on the roll are a mystery, as nothing similar survives. Possibly the artist, an Austrian court painter, mistook hussar nasals for spikes – a theory we explore here. The saddle and horse harness are restored from the tournament gear of Archduke Ferdinand II, of *c.*1550 (Waffensammlung, Vienna). Stirrups are of paddle-shaped Tatar style.

The schematics are [2] from row 1, [3*] row 2 back, [4*] row 4 back, [5] row 2 front, [6] row 5 front, and [7*] row 6 back. Again, pennants marked with asterisks have been partly reconstructed.

D: A HUSSAR *POCZET* IN CAMP, 1620s/30s

The smallest economic unit of the hussars was the *poczet* (retinue). By the mid-17th century, this typically comprised a *towarzysz* (companion), two retainers (*pacholiks*, who formed

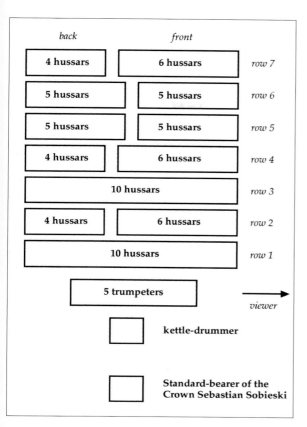

back	front	
4 hussars	6 hussars	row 7
5 hussars	5 hussars	row 6
5 hussars	5 hussars	row 5
4 hussars	6 hussars	row 4
10 hussars		row 3
4 hussars	6 hussars	row 2
10 hussars		row 1

5 trumpeters

→ viewer

kettle-drummer

Standard-bearer of the
Crown Sebastian Sobieski

ABOVE **Arrangement of retinues (*poczets*) of the Company
of Courtiers as shown on the Stockholm Roll. The formation is
led by the Crown Standard-bearer Sebastian Sobieski and six
musicians, followed by a body of 70 hussars, in seven rows each
of ten men. Each row contains either one or two retinues, and in
all 12 differently uniformed retinues are shown. The 'uniforms'
of all 12 retinues are reconstructed in Plates B and C.**

the rear ranks) and perhaps three to six camp servants, plus
six or more horses and several wagons.

Most wagons were of simple wooden construction, similar
to those seen in the Polish countryside today. Valuables were
stored in a weatherproof *skarbnik* or baggage wagon. The
towarzysz had his own tent for sleeping and a second one for
receiving guests, while his *pacholiks* were cramped together
in a single tent and the servants made do with any available
space they could find.

Everyday campaign duties, such as foraging missions,
were largely left to the retainers. For these duties, they
abandoned their lances and took up long firearms –
described usually as muskets – from the wagons. These
muskets were typically stowed in a large holster on the
saddle. Pricelists from Leczyca show that holster-makers
were still making musket holsters in 1649. This holster is
taken from decoration on Zolkiewski's coffin of *c*.1620.

[1] The hussar retainer is loosely based on a 1620s or 30s
painting of the battle of Klushino attributed to Szymon
Boguszowicz. He wears a *kapalin* helmet and a *welens* cape
over his armour – several companies on the Klushino painting

have capes of uniform pattern. His armour still has none of the
brass fittings characteristic of later Polish armour. Before the
adoption of *karwasz* armguards many Polish horsemen wore a
single armour gauntlet on the bridle arm.

[2, 3] Camp servants were 'invisible' men – it is difficult to
find them in the art and literature of the period. Some were
clothed by their masters, in simplified noble garments cut
less generously in the skirts; others were left in peasant
rags. These servants are taken mainly from Della Bella's
sketches of the Polish embassies to Rome in 1633 and Paris
in 1645.

E: THE EVOLUTION OF HUSSAR WINGS

The hussar's wings seem to have evolved from wing devices
seen in Italian and South German heraldry since the 14th
century. In the early 16th century, painted wings or winged
claws began to appear on the asymmetric cavalry shields
favoured in the Balkans **[1]**.

Soon, Serbian and Bosnian *deli* horsemen in Ottoman
service began to attach feathers to their shields in place of
these painted wings **[2]**. This *deli*, in his characteristic leopard,
bear and wolfskin clothing, is based on western and Ottoman
sources from 1530–90. The wing pinned to his shield is not a
whole bird's wing, but rather several layers of feathers.

There is evidence that the Poles imitated the *deli*. An official
account of King Zygmunt III's wedding in 1592 describes a
unit of 60 'delia' parading into Kraków wearing 'tiger and
wolfskins … eagle wings, white and blue plumes and *kopia*
lances'. The Poles also had their own 'chosen men' known as
elears, selected from the bravest hussars, and these affected
the same suicidal bravery of Ottoman *deli* and *serdengeçti*
volunteers. *Elears* played a key role in many actions of the
1580–1629 period, 'opening' the battle with a reckless charge
to disorder the enemy before the main attack.

Depictions of Polish *elears* are rare and they probably
differed little from ordinary hussars. It is only in 1627–28 that
the Dutchman Abraham Booth shows several unarmoured
winged horsemen who may well be *elears*. Our *elear* **[3]** is
based on a watercolour added to Booth's journal (see picture
on page 62). We interpret his wing as of the style worn by
Balkan grenzer cavalry in an Ottoman costume book of
c.1590 (Codex Vindob. 8626, ONB, Vienna). The frameless
wing is strapped loosely around the neck. The rest of the
elear's equipment is more typical of Polish cossacks than
hussars, and he may be a member of the Lisowski cossacks,
who began to call themselves *elears* in the 1620s.

This type of wing, worn on the shoulders, did not survive long.
Soon after the Balkan shield was abandoned, the hussar went
over to a frame wing attached to the left side of the saddle. A
possible 'missing link' in this migration **[4]** may be depicted in
Merian's fancy dress Hungarian heroes who took part in the
Stuttgart carousel of 1616. They appear to be wearing frame-
wings attached to their left arm, in place of a shield.

Ultimately the frame wing switched from the saddle to the
back. **[5]** The first clear image of such a wing comes only in
1645, with Colonel Szczodrowski – a member of the Polish
delegation to Paris (see page 21). Unfortunately, the
contemporary illustrations do not show how his ostrich wing
is attached. We reconstruct it with the help of the Skokloster
wing (pages 28–29). The colours of Szczodrowski's clothing
are taken from Della Bella's sketches and the official French
government account of the event.

LEFT **A winged *elear* scout, in a watercolour added to Booth's *Journal* of 1632, in the Gdansk state archive. At this date, the *elear*'s role of 'opening the battle' was passing from hussars to unarmoured *kozak* formations, such as the famous Lisowczyks (or Lisowski Cossacks) who began to call themselves *elears*. This has confused later generations of historians, who have forgotten the unique role of the original hussar *elears*.**

F: HUSSAR *TOWARZYSZ*, c.1680s

Much of our traditional image of the hussar was created by the collection of hussar equipment at Podhorce Palace. This gear is said to have been worn at Vienna in 1683 by the company of Crown Grand Hetman Stanislaw Jablonowski, though its use in the 18th century is better attested.

Hussar armour is usually classified into an early or 'Older type' (*typ starszy*), with a distinct ridge down the middle of each element of the suit, which Bochenski dated provisionally to 1640–75, and a 'Younger type' (*typ mlodszy*) of c.1675–c.1730, which had cleaner lines and often dispensed with the gorget. Bochenski's datings have acquired the status of gospel, but may be incorrect by several decades.

[1] Our central figure wears a Podhorce suit of 'Younger type', now at the Hermitage Museum. His zupan is taken from the garment captured at Narva in 1700, while his boots are from the Livrustkammaren. His single wing is covered with plain leather, and is the most common surviving type of wing, easily outnumbering the variety lined with velvet and brass, most of which are modern replicas. Though worn singly rather than in pairs, the extra-long feathers at the top give these wings a particularly spectacular appearance.

The detail of the wing [2] is based on examples in the Kraków National Museum, which are similar to those from Podhorce. The feathers are sewn between two leather-covered wooden battens. The twin fastening points are reinforced with iron, and slot into fittings on the armour backplate.

[3] A hussar armour of the 'Older type'. A handful of such suits survive, with almost identical decoration – copious amounts of brass strip applied over the steel surfaces. Though splendid from a distance, the decoration [4] is quite primitive, consisting of simple punchwork and engraving that even a village smith could achieve.

The most common breast appliqué was the stylized knight's cross [5]. It is often said this was the mark of a noble, but since it also appears on lower-quality armour made for rear-rankers, it was probably no more than a nationality mark – compare the cross on most Polish standards. It is thought that appliqués depicting the Virgin Mary with Child [6] were connected with a chivalric Order of the Immaculate Conception, which King Wladyslaw IV attempted to set up in 1633–37. But they may just be standard Catholic imagery: a few surviving appliqués depict St George and Archangel Michael, and these doubtless refer to recruitment in the Commonwealth's Orthodox eastern provinces or even Russia.

Note the huge length of the *koncerz* sword [7]. Its awkwardness has led some authorities to suggest it was no more than a parade weapon; in reality, it was especially useful during pursuit. By the late 17th century the Polish sabre [8] had reached the pinnacle of its evolution. It now had a fully closed hilt to protect the knuckles, and a thumb-ring on the guard to speed recovery of the weapon between blows.

Polish hairstyles altered greatly over the period: from the 'flat mohican' style popular in the early 17th century [9], to a style peculiar to the 1640s and 50s [10] with front and sides shaved and only the back left to grow (sometimes very long as here) and the monk-like tonsure [11] favoured by Sobieski, which was widely copied from the 1670s.

G: THE CHARGE OF PRINCE ALEXANDER SOBIESKI'S COMPANY AT VIENNA, 1683

At about 4pm on 12 September 1683, King Jan Sobieski released 3,000 Polish hussars towards Vienna and destiny. However, prior to the hussar's most famous charge, the Polish king tested that the ground was suitable for cavalry by sending out the hussar company of his infant son Alexander (1677–1714) on a sacrificial charge towards the Turkish lines.

The eyewitness Dyakowski saw the company disappear into a cloud of gun-smoke and dust, catching an occasional glimpse of the unit's flag 'which was of half black and half hot-yellow silk, on which was a white eagle'. The 19th-century Austrian historian Anton Dolleczek mentions that this unit had black and yellow lance pennants. This has not been confirmed in 17th-century sources, although black and yellow is a common combination, and pennants usually matched the company flag. A simple chequered pennant is the most common design seen in the art of Sobieski's reign.

The flag [1] carried by the *chorazy* (standard bearer) is reconstructed from other 17th-century flags, with Sobieski's 'Janina' clan badge (a Balkan shield) added on the eagle's breast. His cape is a Crimean camel hair *burka*.

The *towarzysz* [2] is based on the central figure in Altomonte's colossal painting of the battle commissioned by Sobieski in 1684 but not completed until the 1690s. We have removed some of Altomonte's unhistorical additions, but left the *karwasze* armguards with mittens and armour cuisses (thigh guards). Surviving hussar armour suits are not normally made with cuisses, yet Beauplan (1640s), Gramont (1664) and Brulig (1683) mention hussars wearing them. Possibly these were from obsolete western cuirassier armours fitted to hussar suits by their owners.

The *pacholik* (retainer) [3] is taken from German/Austrian depictions of the battle, which frequently show hussars wearing caps rather than helmets. His cheaper equipment includes a wolfskin.

The trumpeter [4] is based on one of the few surviving battle-paintings from Podhorce by De Baan, dating from c.1660. He is one of a pair of unarmoured trumpeters accompanying a company of armoured hussars. The sheepskin-lined cap is again typical of retainers and camp servants.

LEFT **Hussars of Duke Janusz Radziwill at Kiev in 1651 during the Ukrainian Cossack Rebellion. The two company flags have simple knight's cross devices and ball-shaped finials, and are dwarfed by the hussar lances with their long pennants. There were no regulations on the design of hussar standards. Traditionally they were larger than the standards of lighter grades of Polish cavalry, and had either a rounded fly or two tails. They were carried on a staff of about 3.5m length, shorter than the 5m hussar lance, but more richly painted and not hollowed out as this would reduce strength. There can be little doubt that the cross born on most Polish cavalry standards was intended as a national emblem. (From an 18th-century copy of a now-lost sketch by Radziwill's court artist, Abraham van Westerveldt)**

INDEX

References to illustrations are shown in **bold**. Plates are shown with page and caption locators in brackets.